THE SEA HAS WINGS

THE SEA HAS WINGS

FRANKLIN RUSSELL
photographs by LES LINE

A Sunrise Book | E. P. Dutton Co., Inc. | New York | 1973

Outerbridge & Lazard,
a subsidiary of E. P. Dutton & Co., Inc.
Published simultaneously in Canada by
Clarke, Irwin & Company Limited, Toronto and Vancouver
ISBN: 0-87690-097-X
Library of Congress Catalog Card Number: 72-94696

For Jack and Rita Russell,
keepers of the light and the birdlife
on Machias Seal Island, Bay of Fundy

CONTENTS

One: Preface 11
Two: The Waiting Islands 54
Three: The Outer World 65
Four: The Quest for Survival 75
Five: Spring of the Seabird 102
Six: The Young Seabirds 148
Seven: The Killing Country 156
Eight: Finale 181

Photographs

I: The Gannetry 16
II: The Gullery 80
III: The Puffinry 112
IV: The Ternery 160

THE SEA HAS WINGS

ONE: PREFACE

I

Once, many years ago, I stood on an empty island where the wind blew so strongly that the earth underfoot trembled with the crashing of distant waves. I could scarcely stand against the strength of the wind shrieking through the surrounding spruces. The island was so desolate, so completely lifeless and lonely, surrounded by the rush and roar of the sea, that it was difficult to imagine it a center for scores of thousands of seabirds. When ready, they would come out of the sea to transform this place into an uproar of movement, sound, and smell. I leaned into a wind screeching over crusted snow. Underfoot lay the tunnels and burrows of some of these birds. Ahead, the island came to an abrupt end where cliffs dropped vertically into the sea. In that ice-hung place was the summer home of multitudes of sea creatures where they perched precariously a hundred feet or more above the waters of the Atlantic.

Nonetheless, this empty, desolate place became alive in my imagination. I was possessed by the ghosts of its departed creatures and by memories of the many summers I had spent with them. The winter wind might be deafening but I could easily conjure up other sounds —the wheedling cries of kittiwakes, the deep-throated roar of masses of murres, the querulous shrieks of herring gulls, the gargling cries of gannets. I could hear the sweeping, wild cries of petrels rushing like points of light through the island darkness, listen to an imagination of screeching terns overhead, the strange songs of laughing gulls, the croaks of puffins.

All this was easy enough to conjure up. Seabirds are the most purely dramatic of all winged creatures. The others live in the *shelter* of their land but the seabird lives in the hands of the wind, in the grip of the full force of wind and sea combined. I could imagine them now, flung across a revolutionary constellation of wind and rain and ice, of giant waves and clashing currents. Out there, buried hundreds, even thousands, of miles deep in the spume of the storm, millions of them were riding the wind, fighting for their lives. They are, I believe, the toughest forms of life on earth, and it would be a churlish fellow whose imagination was not thoroughly captured by them.

But I would concede that they are not immediately the most colorful creatures. There are people who think seabirds are the dullest of earth's animals. These must be people, I assume, who do not see them in their infinite subtleties; the texture of feathers, the cant of wings as they land on lichen-studded rocks, the symmetrical grace of their falls to earth from high sky stations, their frenzied chases in the troughs of waves, their motionless vigils in trees. To appreciate the seabird, both word and picture are needed to describe him even if the major part of his life remains buried at sea, like the iceberg, nine-tenths beyond sight or comprehension.

Men had already devoted their lives to studying a single species and could, at best, summarize their knowledge in a slender book. One man who had spent twenty years studying a single species said helplessly to me once, "I now know I will never live long enough to even begin to understand these creatures."

In watching such a secret world, so largely private from the prying eyes of man, I cannot hope to do more than hint at the scope and quality of their lives.

II

Long before I stood on that desolate island, long before I had any interest in seabirds, I had traveled for years without developing much understanding of the seabird world. True, I had watched with admiration as the graceful albatross planed Pacific waves and appreciated how beautifully sea and creature had become part of each other. I had seen the delicate Mother Carey's chickens, the petrels, dancing on the water like little girls on points in ballet. I had seen boobies slipping with deadly accuracy across dead calm waters to snatch flying fish in midair. I had watched kittiwakes being driven north by Atlantic storms, a thousand miles from anywhere, and had seen Arctic terns sweeping along the coast of Africa on their way from Arctic to Antarctic. But this world of the seabird, glimpsed so fleetingly and spread over such vast distances, could not be brought into a single, comprehensible picture. I had given up trying to make much sense of it.

But then, accidentally, I found myself wandering through the territories and seasons of the northeastern coast of North America, a shore where millions of seabirds gather to breed every year in countless island cities. Here, I found not merely a necklace of seabird cities strung along an infinitely diversified shore, but also a world of great tides, of hissing currents colliding and boiling up dense mists, of seas filled with fish and plankton. Here, if a man were prepared to travel far enough, and wait long enough, he might see these sea creatures close up, watch them during their brief domestic time ashore when necessity made them tolerate the watcher.

In this territory which stretches roughly from the Gulf of Maine as far north as you care to travel (the seabirds have colonized this world almost to the edge of the ice pack), there are hundreds of seabird congregations, some of them numbering a few dozen, others running into the scores and hundreds of thousands. The largest bird city contains more than a million creatures packed together on an island in a kind of Jovian nightmare.

In the years of wandering this shore, I have developed a special kind of enthusiasm for the seabirds and have come to realize that I admire them immensely. Their ingenuity in surviving in a mercilessly hard world, their toughness, their diversity of habit and form, the drama of their activities, all are the ingredients of my growing admiration. The sea is not only filled with wings. It is also a secret place which offers a handsome living to any creature ingenious enough to seek it out.

III

To watch the activities of seabirds is something more than mere observation of a drama of natural history; it is a study in primeval personalities. The watcher vicariously becomes a participant as he is drawn into their world. No species of seabird closely resembles any other in behavior. While all seabirds respond to the changes of seasons, moving north, south, east, and west in traditional migrations, there is no agreement among them *when* to move, *where* to breed; no agreement about how to handle storm, ice, prolonged drought, lack of food; practically no commonality about their hunting or the rearing of their youngsters.

Seabirds are a small and independent example of the diversity of life itself. They are not merely an education to watch but also a drama, a comic opera, a tragedy, an entertainment played out on a vast stage. To describe their complexity of habit and to encompass the size of their world and its many contradictions demand special treatment. It is easy enough to type out an ornithological description of numbers, movements, and the enumeration of species. All this work has been done. But such information says nothing about the strength of the wind at midnight in the deep ocean where there are hundreds of thousands of wanderers. It tells little of the impact of the hurricane or the unexpected freeze and ignores the joyous spirit that must grip seabirds when they smother the surface of the waters, penetrate its submarine depths, and rise hundreds of feet in the air in great dances that precede lovemaking.

This ocean of wings needs to be seen through humanistic eyes, with the odd glance at the bird guide to check an ornithological fact. Our journey into the seabirds' world, therefore, goes from vignette to vignette as we try to follow their private lives with camera and pen to a point of revelation.

IV

But where to begin? Any year of seabirds is dramatic, any month is fascinating. Let us look for them in January from a seagoing ship, or helicopter, or light airplane. It is possible to sail for weeks and see only a handful of birds. You may fly for days in search of them and find nothing. The sea from the Maine coast to Labrador seems empty. Pack ice clogs the Straits of Belle Isle and spills out into the Gulf of St. Lawrence. The ocean has frozen along the shores of Newfoundland's east coast and tumbling gray seas march in endless lines toward shores almost permanently shrouded in winter haze. To find the seabirds now is either a matter of luck or requires a well-informed knowledge of their habits.

Abruptly, the airplane heels and turns around the rocky shores of a small island. There, crammed together in their tens of thousands, are eider ducks filling a few acres of open water in the ice. They are floating over a favorite shellfish hunting ground and keep the water open by their massed presence and activity.

The airplane heads out to sea since we are now suddenly confident that the birds *can* be found. And sure enough, there they are, a thousand puffins riding together in a loose-knit raft off the southern shores of Nova Scotia. Small groups of murres scud along against the wind on the Grand Banks where fleets of European fishing vessels are busy scouring the bottom of the sea for everything they can catch. We find gulls standing like glass statues on frozen estuarine mud and squabbling in tumultuous throngs wherever upsurging currents are bringing young fish to the surface. Here and there, lone guillemots show white body patches as they slip along an empty shore while far out to sea in the Gulf of Maine a pair of razorbills floats in the endless swell.

Once, when I was riding out a storm on the Grand Banks on a Canadian dragger—one of those powerful fishing boats which pull great open-mouthed nets across the bottom—I went out on deck to watch the waves. The ferocity of the storm, seen from the .level of the waves themselves because the dragger rides so low, was frightening. I could not help remembering how many Newfoundland and European fishing vessels have been destroyed at sea in such weather. But despite the strength of the wind and the height of the waves, I saw a tight clot of birds speeding along the trough of a wave. As they came near the pitching dragger, they suddenly realized that they must swerve to avoid the vessel; and they came up out of the trough, caught the full force of the wind on their wings, and in one incredibly

(continued on page 49)

THE GANNETRY

At Percé, a village at the tip of the Gaspé Peninsula in the Province of Quebec, stand two islands that are famous for their birdlife. Percé Rock, a chunk of stone with perpendicular sides and shaped like a gigantic ship pointed toward shore, hosts kittiwakes and cormorants on its broad flat top. Nearby Bonaventure Island, far more hospitable with its open fields and dense boreal forest, is one of the greatest seabird refuges on Earth. Its towering, seaward-facing cliffs fall sheer into the Gulf of St. Lawrence and are lined with thousands of gannets that constantly pour back and forth, to and from their offshore fishing grounds. The sound of the sea hissing at the foot of the cliffs and the gargling of gannet voices combine to create an intimidating atmosphere.

The nests of the gannets are crude mounds of material roughly piled up from the sloping rock terraces. They appear to be insecure refuges—and gannet eggs and nestlings sometimes do tumble into the sea. But the loss, unnoticed in a colony of such magnitude, is a small price to pay for security from nearly all enemies. There have been foxes and other predatory mammals on Bonaventure, but they can have little effect on a congregation of birds so well placed at the edge of the Atlantic.

From the top of the Bonaventure cliffs an observer looks down on the sailing gannets and sees them as if he were also a flying bird. He sees their dramatic arrival at the nest, great wings braking the hurtling body to a landing on a ledge only a few inches wide. He sees their departure as they pour away in a steady stream for rich fishing grounds, though one member of each pair always remains at the nest. Everywhere he looks there is movement and excitement and a sense of unity with the vastness of the sea that stretches to the horizon.

The face of the gannet is too striking to be an accidental creation. The eyes swivel in their sockets, their golden color catching the light, while the beak opens to reveal a red interior—features that are necessary to the complex system of communication between birds.

[*Overleaf*]
Pairs of gannets cement their bond with an extraordinary series of displays, grotesque yet oddly touching. They face each other, stretching their necks, and though they may be standing on a ledge only six inches wide, they tap their beaks together with rapid, saberlike motions, all the while flailing their wings and bowing. Frequently they will fall off their insecure footings. In the sequence of pictures on the following pages, one gannet holds in its beak a small feather that is somehow significant to its ceremonial dance.

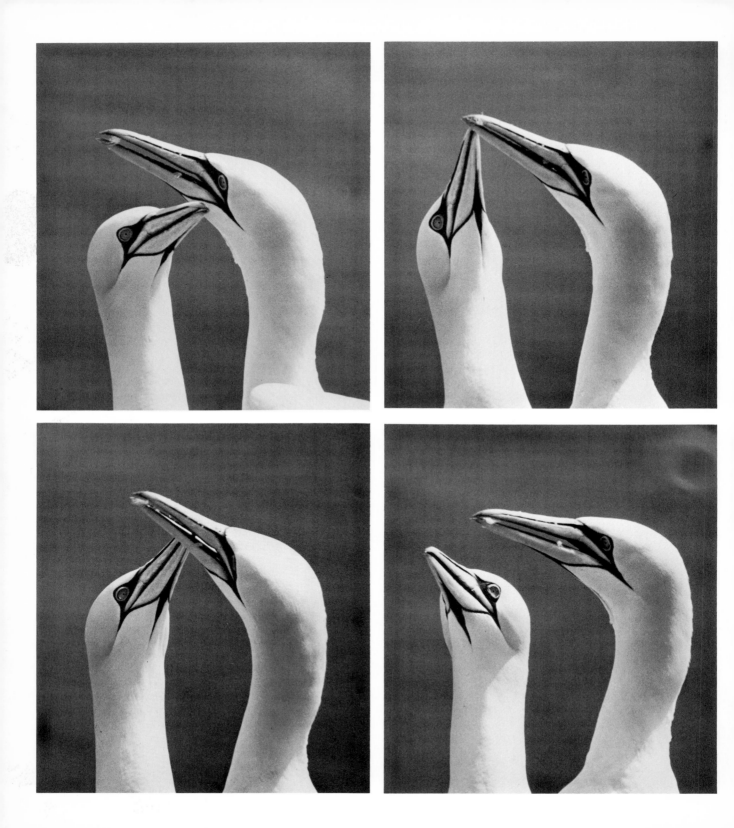

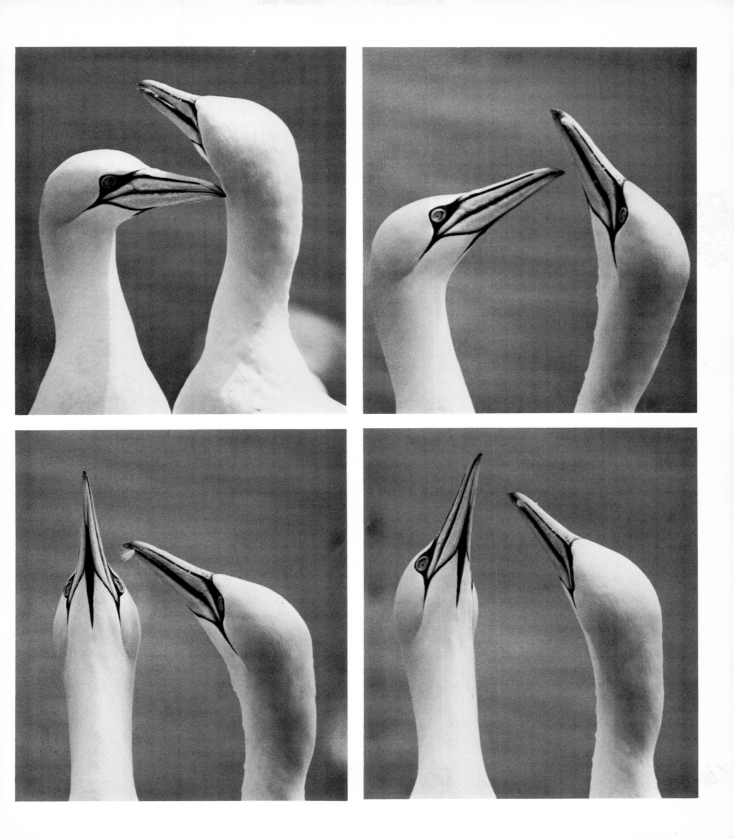

Paired gannets bring bunches of seaweed to the nest site and pass them back and forth in displays that may go on for half an hour at a time. Perhaps there is a connection between the gathering of food and the use of nesting material for display. Gannets do not feed each other at the nest, as do some other seabirds, and the seaweed may be a sublimated material.

No space is wasted at the gannetry, and every movement is governed by the amount of room that is available. Each nesting bird sits just beyond reach of the formidable beaks of its neighbors. And although paired gannets will sit close in comradely attitudes, should another bird attempt to move past, it arouses immediate hostility.

Bonaventure Island is host to black-legged kittiwakes that cling to nests fastened to the vertical cliffs, and a small population of common murres, whose true home is much farther north, beginning at Funk Island off the northeastern coast of Newfoundland where (following pages) more than 1,500,000 of their kind breed.

The gannet is graceful and majestic on the wing, but clumsy on land, and thus it selects for its breeding places those cliffs that have full exposure to the wind. When conditions are right, a gannet is able to settle gently on its nest when returning from the sea. But if the wind is wrong, particularly if it is calm, landing can be a crisis. Wings outspread, suggesting a bomber settling on the runway, the cross-shaped bird approaches the cliff, frantically braking as it passes over the serried rows of brooding birds. . . .

Flapping its wings against the direction of flight in an attempt to decrease its speed, it plunges toward its colleagues. But there is no opportunity to make a creditable landing, and the onrushing gannet smashes into the upright heads in a rippling series of collisions that only appear disastrous for both parties. . . .

Finally, in a flurry of wingbeats, the landing bird itself falls, sometimes turning tail over head or—in this instance—plunging its chest hard onto a sharp stone. Then, not at all perturbed, the birds behind it recovered and equally undisturbed, the gannet rises, flails its wings a few times, and settles down to incubate.

To leave the gannetry can also pose a problem, since the gannet cannot take immediate flight like a gull. If its nest is on a shelf, the bird can simply jump into the void. But if its nest is on the densely packed clifftop, there is little room to move among the brooding birds, and its takeoff must be carefully modulated. First, as if announcing intent, the gannet raises its neck high, points its beak vertically for a few moments, then lifts its wings. This seems to cause consternation among its neighbors, and the closest birds may threaten to attack and even seize its wing tips. If there is adequate wind coming off the sea, the gannet can lift itself off the ground after a few quick steps forward. If there is no wind, the bird wanting to depart is in a quandary. In front of it is a sea of hostile faces, awaiting its move. But it must be made. Stretching its wings, the gannet charges forward, flailing, knocking over any bird in its path, until it reaches the brink.

The gannet is a heavy-bodied, strong-flying bird and—like an arrow shot from a bow —is unable to change its course suddenly. Thus a gust of wind, smashing against the rock face and ballooning up under its wings, may bring disaster in the form of the impaling branches of a dead clifftop spruce.

Every gannetry has its contingent of herring gulls that regularly watch from the sky or from nearby crags. The gull will never challenge the much larger gannet. Instead, it is an eternal opportunist, grabbing a dropped fish or snatching an egg or small chick that has been left unguarded, perhaps by a parent that has lost its mate. When gannets and gulls are on the wing together, the observer is rewarded by a chance to compare the styles of two master fliers. While the gull balances on the updraft off the cliffs, the gannet rushes past, alternately sailing and then rapidly beating its long wings.

So many of the displays of the gannet seem to express human emotions that it is hard not to attribute special feelings to these great seabirds. When the paired gannets change places during the incubation of their egg, the relieving bird stands tall on the nest, raises its wings and neck, and points its beak vertically. The significance of this display is buried too deep in gannet history for man to understand, but it seems a triumphant gesture by a bird that has survived against both the will of the sea and the desires of its enemies on land.

quick movement, they shot overhead like bullets, missing stay wires, radio antennas, and deck ventilators by scant feet.

It does not seem to matter what the weather is doing. The seabird occupies his position in the water world without regard for how hard the wind blows. I was on the dragger in January and had to marvel at the precision with which each population of these birds has fitted into the maritime world. The older gulls, and the ducks, would never be found in such a storm, holding fast to limited and familiar hunting grounds, but the true seabirds, like the murres and puffins, wander across hundreds of miles of open ocean from one food source to another. This may be random wandering, but I doubt it. The accuracy with which the seabirds arrive at their feeding places cannot be accidental. Even in the storm, the fish are feeding, and, sure enough, there are the seabirds, feeding on them. But the sheer size and the apparent featurelessness of the seascape remains daunting to the human watcher.

Within sixty days, this bleak winter picture changes radically as the seabird year gradually becomes visible. It begins tumultuously in the lap of the Labrador current, centered around a desolate chunk of granite—Funk Island—still half-obscured in the vapors of winter. The island was once the western Atlantic headquarters of the great auk, wiped out there in the eighteenth century. Now, in the freezing cold (the sea is only a degree or so above freezing), it is surrounded by more than a million common murres which, under pallid, often snow-filled skies, are beginning mad, prenuptial water dances and joy flights.

The murres are making a ballet out of this month of March, not only at Funk Island but also under the high cliffs of Cape St. Mary's, off southern Newfoundland, at Baccalieu Island on the eastern coast, and off a string of islands along the north shore of the Gulf of St. Lawrence. They are at Quebec's Bonaventure Island too, and at odd points along the coast of Nova Scotia.

The murres, relatives of the extinct great auk, are close relatives of puffin, guillemot, and razorbill, all of them auks. Their great flights are not poetic, of course, but coldly biologic. The auks need to speed up or to unify their sexual maturity. The spirit of the season moves through the early breeding murres and passes on to the puffins, those oddly beautiful, strange, clumsy, graceful seabirds that some people perversely describe as parrotlike. Actually, they resemble nothing except puffins because there are no other birds like them anywhere. They, too, are transformed as they move closer to shore and begin swarming water chases and flights around Great Island off Newfoundland's eastern shore, at Perroquet Island in the northern Gulf of St. Lawrence, and as far south as Machias Seal, a lonely island in the northern Gulf of Maine which stands guard in the opening of the Bay of Fundy.

These are the two common auks. The other two auks, the guillemots and razorbills, are scarcely visible at all as they begin to ease themselves out of winter servitude. The razorbills can be seen near some groups of puffins and later they will go ashore at some places with the puffins and, at Machias Seal, will mingle with them on rocky breeding grounds.

The auks have opened the year but it is the herring gulls who will come to dominate it. They have made a special place for themselves by the sea. They are not seabirds in the strictest sense because, unlike the other seabirds emerging from the sea, they are *entering* it. From a thousand mainland points they are flying out to island breeding places. This movement is less a study in exuberance, in auklike joy, than it is an experiment in caution. They nest at hundreds of points along the coast and on scores of islands. The greatest colony of them is accessible, at Kent Island, in the southern Bay of Fundy. The gulls will occupy it like a division of battle-hardened soldiers who have learned that all islands may conceal deadly enemies, not the least of them being man himself.

There are other gulls less visible and more specialized. The austere great black-backed gulls, really voluntary immigrants from the low Arctic, and masters of the harsh conditions of the north, are now moving into easier southern climates. They appear to be living amicably with the herring gulls but they may, in fact, be destroying them.

The blackbacks are moving south but the laughing gulls, beautiful black-headed creatures with one of the most distinctive cries of the sea, are moving north into the Gulf of Maine. Blackbacks and laughing gulls meet, along with the herring gull, at Petit Manan Island and there will briefly reenact their small part of the seabird year.

The gannets, regal additions to the cast of characters being built up in this marine world, offer no exuberance, no ceremonies as they come into their breeding territory. They fly up directly from the Gulf of Mexico, or coastal Florida, and land immediately, roughly two hundred and fifty thousand birds spread between Bonaventure Island, Bird Rock in the middle of the Gulf of St. Lawrence, Cape St. Mary's, Baccalieu, and finally—their northern bastion—Funk Island. The gannets, in common with all other seabirds, are visible only to the watcher who knows where to expect them, and when.

The eider ducks are now gathered in large groups called "rafts" because they pack so densely together. The black-and-white plumage of the males stands out starkly among the more numerous brown-colored females. They are in no hurry to begin breeding and they will let most of the other birds go ashore before they begin to move toward their islands in search of nesting places buried deep in thick undergrowth that has not, as yet, begun growing.

It is impossible to be present simultaneously at all the scenes of action at this time, but I have seen a few. In the mornings, when I was offshore in fishing boats almost anywhere along any coast, there was constant inshore movement of all seabirds. The puffins appeared abruptly out of the mist of the Gulf of St. Lawrence, fifty miles off the Quebec coast, all headed north and directly for the shoreline where, later, they would breed on islands there. By that time, the murres have gone, at least in their large wintering flocks, from the Grand Banks southeast of Newfoundland. All their flights tend to be northern, toward the eastern shore islands, particularly Funk Island. It may be my imagination, but there is a purposiveness about this time that speaks of the new season coming. The birds are not waiting any more. They *know* where they are going precisely.

All this is visible to the watcher in movement everywhere and excitement everywhere. If very lucky, that most mysterious of all seabirds, the Leach's petrel, may reveal himself. But more likely, at this early stage in the year, he will still be far offshore, waiting for his opportunity to come to land. He is a day bird on the high seas, though, and stragglers may sometimes be seen a hundred miles offshore. But they must become night birds when they get close to their breeding islands along the shore. This is their ancient method of avoiding their land-loving enemies.

The seabirds are a constant series of studies in contrast. The petrel, with its dusky black plumage and its close relationship to the albatross, makes sharp counterpoint to other great oceanic wanderers who are also making their approach to the breeding territories of the Maritimes. These are the Arctic terns. With their capacity to fly across great distances of open sea, they have even evolved to look like petrels (or perhaps it is the other way around). Unlike the petrels, however, they are visible and noisy in their conquest of the sea and land.

Some of them, now deep into their flight across the Atlantic, are coming from as far south as Antarctic coasts and will skirt the coast of Africa to reach their maritime region. Thousands of them will not even stop in this territory but will press on farther north. There, in the Arctic, they will stake out territories that are geographically as far-removed from their wintering grounds in the Antarctic as is possible.

V

All of this movement and excitement is more than a natural history drama or a study in the survival of one winter. It is the triumphant survival of the seabirds in the face of almost three hundred years of persecution. These great prenuptial flights, these nocturnal migrations, these oceanic dashes for island refuges are performed by descendants of the victims of ancient massacres. They are the generational heirs of birds that escaped thousands of eager muskets in the eighteenth and nineteenth centuries when men shot seabirds wherever and whenever they saw them. They have survived generations of fishermen who baited millions of fish hooks with seabird flesh. They have survived the systematic harvesting of millions of their eggs taken by the coastal people from almost every accessible island every year, eggs which for generations made fishermen's omelettes—"*Real* omelettes," say fishermen's wives, "that can hold a man's hunger off while he's working all day in the boat"—which were preserved for use for the rest of the year, and which, for countless generations of Indians, were one of the most important staples. They have outlasted the murderous expeditions that took twenty and thirty thousand of their bodies a day from some islands. They have outbred a harvesting of their flesh which saw the food lockers of schooners fishing the Grand Banks, the Labrador coast, the Gulf of St. Lawrence jammed with their salted bodies. They are still in their world whereas the whalermen who once killed them are long since gone.

They have outbred the searching guns of three centuries of starving coastal folk, outlived the demand for hundreds of thousands of gallons of oil rendered from their bodies for cooking and for lighting lamps from New Brunswick to Portugal, from Nova Scotia to Scotland. They have beaten the musket, the flintlock, the double-barreled shotgun, the pump-action, the automatic. They have withstood cannons mounted in punts which slaughtered two and three hundred birds with one shot. They have endured, summer after bloody summer, the depredations of Indians, Vikings, Portuguese, Dutchmen, British, Canadians, Americans.

They have survived so handsomely partly because of man's protective laws, partly because his habits, appetite, and awareness are changing.

By the end of April, between five and six million seabirds are in place on their island metropolises. Then they become characters in our saga of how the sea has sprouted wings and made a small miracle of natural history for all to enjoy.

TWO: THE WAITING ISLANDS

I

Next to the great freedom of the open seas, the prime fact of the seabird year is the island. Only the island can give the seabird the refuge it needs from a mainland teeming with enemies. Only the island can provide the aircraft-carrier landing field strategically placed among convenient feeding grounds. It is no accident that the islands chosen by the seabirds rise from relatively shallow waters where fish come to breed and feed and so become summer victims of the seabirds.

Each of these islands is outwardly similar to every other one, but their inward atmospheres, or personalities, are radically different. Each island has been taken by its seabird populations and molded by them into a series of microcosmic worlds. I hesitate to use the word "cities" again to describe them, and yet that is what so many of them are—hurrying, bustling, crowded, noisy, dirty, cooperative, quarrelsome, and spectacular.

Each species of birds puts its distinct imprint on its island, sometimes to the near exclusion of all other species. The Arctic terns have managed to dominate Machias Seal in the most southern part of our territory, and have covered almost every available square yard of its treeless, grass-cloaked surface with their nests and territories. They occupy land which is ideal for the burrow-constructing puffins but none of these larger birds has been given permission by the terns to go anywhere near this delectable breeding ground. Instead, they are grudgingly permitted to occupy the masses of jumbled rocks which face the open ocean side of the island and to make their nests deep under huge boulders. But even there, on odd patches of soil or sand, even on hollows of bare rocks, the terns have spread out to build their nests.

The terns imprint their island with the grace of their beautiful flight movements, yet this quality is made sharp edged by their bad tempers and their willingness to attack anything in defense of their territories. Thus, we walk across the island under a canopy of beautiful, buoyant, graceful creatures screeching the worst kind of obscenities at us. But they have come to agreement with man on their island and they return to their nests seconds after he has passed. He is an interloper but he has also become their savior.

Years ago, careless or heedless lighthouse keepers let their dogs run wild on Machias Seal and the dogs found great sport smashing up eggs and running down fledgling terns. Gulls from the mainland made regular sorties for eggs and young in such numbers that the terns could not repel them. But now, a new breed of lighthouse keeper has grown in response to the concern of conservationists, and prowling gulls are likely to be met with rifle bullets. Jack Russell, a Canadian lighthouse-man, has become a protector and observer and recorder of tern and puffin, and so has helped to make the tern world safer.

Machias Seal, like so many of the coastal islands, is nothing more than a scrap of low-lying, utterly bare land, its green sward a brilliant decoration in the blue sea on fine days. Like many of the other islands, it is so low that winter waves sometimes break clean over it. Even summer storms are perilous for terns nesting near its shores. This is one reason why terns have no difficulty resettling themselves on an egg that has been moved a dozen feet by wind or wave, or digging their eggs out from under wave-borne debris or sand, and settling back immediately into the routine of incubation.

The atmosphere of each island is changed by tiny differences in topography, or plant life, or location in relation to where the food supplies are, or by the concern of men for preserving the birds on them. On nearby Petit Manan, which lies about a dozen miles south-west of Machias Seal and closely resembles it in appearance, the American lighthousemen have developed their own affection for the terns and their guns keep the overpowering presence of the gulls from obliterating the terns altogether.

But Petit Manan has one tiny difference which changes its atmosphere completely. The terns cannot dominate its grassy area because part of it, near the lighthouse buildings, is shaped into a hollow, shallow bowl, and this has encouraged a thick growth of tall grasses. This one fact has given a chancy home to several hundred laughing gulls whose roadways and tunnels run through the thick grasses to their nests. There, the screeching terns and the musical cries of the laughing gulls give the island a subtle touch of difference.

In dramatic juxtaposition is nearby Green Island where the guns of men cannot reach the gulls. There, in half a dozen acres of wave-roiled gravel bars, an ephemeral lagoon, and some thick jungles of angelica, not a single tern makes its nest. Instead, this is the territory of the herring gulls and the great black-backed gulls. Somehow, the eider ducks have reached agreement with the gulls, although gulls love duck eggs, and the ducks skitter in and out of the undergrowth, streaming out into the lagoon followed by their trails of bustling nestlings.

II

Each island is different. I can easily attribute human characteristics to nearly all of them. Some are dour and cheerless; others are bright and optimistic. Their moods and characters change with the seasons. Funk Island, in a good breeding year, can be an explosion of new life roaring its success to the skies over the Labrador current. In a year of uncertain food supplies, it can be a place of sustaining and almost unbearable tragedy where the crippled and the dead lie everywhere. The chaos and uproar of one island contrasts with another which is quiet and brooding in the eternal sea wind.

Bonaventure Island first caught my interest in seabirds. By the happy chance of its placement close to the Quebec shore, it is by far the easiest to reach. Scores of thousands of people had landed on the island ahead of me so there was no special feeling of the unknown when I made my first visit. Nonetheless, the island arranged an almost theatrical display of bird life for me. As does everybody else, I set out from the mainland side of the island to walk the width of the island to reach its open seaside where the thousands of seabirds are gathered at the great cliffs there. The island itself is a great wedge-shaped chunk of land covering several hundred acres, its blunt side facing the open ocean with spectacular cliffs, its spruce forests sloping down to its western shoreline where men once attempted to farm the island and where the half-dozen residents still live.

I set out before dawn's light to walk the track uphill through the woods. Before I entered the woods, I could literally hear the *breathing* of the mainland, a combination of countless indistinguishable sounds, the hiss of automobile tires, the muted cries of cattle, the sound of men packed together. But as I entered the woods, the sound of the mainland diminished and died and I was surrounded by utter stillness. The walk to the cliffs coincided with the wakening of the land birds in the woods and the first cries of resident sparrows sounded brightly in the darkness. Touches of light filtered through the thick canopy of trees over me, an external world awakening while I remained in the separate world of the sleeping forest. Then, ahead, another sound, a different kind of life massed together, a sustained and quiet cacophony of gannets facing another day on their cliffs. Just as I came within a score of paces of leaving the woods, a patch of blue sky showed at the end of the woodland corridor, and set right in the middle of it was the black cross of a gannet holding himself still in the wind.

Bonaventure is a true haven for both man and animal because of its proximity to the shore. I have frequently stretched out in its tall summer grasses, surrounded by its quiet, breathing presence, and dimly heard the sounds of the mainland—automobile horns, tires screaming, shouts, shots—the noises of civilization. But that narrow strip of water separating island and mainland is the salvation of the seabird. And when the sea freezes occasionally, and foxes and raccoons come across the ice to prowl the island, they find nothing. The seabirds are far out to sea, and safe.

The island is a haven, but not just for seabirds. Frequently, thousands of redpolls and crossbills, snow buntings, and sparrows come to the island to spend days or weeks there feeding on grass and tree seeds. Bonaventure seems to be a magnet for dovekies, the smallest of the auks, pigeon sized and Greenland based, who crowd around its shores for protection against high winds and seas. It is a haven for migrants and wanderers, for eider ducks, mergansers, old squaws, goldeneyes, murres, and willow ptarmigans.

But it is the gannets which give Bonaventure its unique imprint. They cluster in groups, mass together in hundreds, line up in serried ranks along the faults in the strata lines of the ocean cliffs. They occupy knolls and rockfaces and gravel beds practically all around the island. They stud the blue or gray sky like accusatory crosses, riding that steady and apparently perennial sea wind with all the assurance of manned gliders. Their gaggling voices are sounds that have come in from far distant seas, guttural cries of the primeval concentrated in this place.

The eastern cliffs are among the most sensational bird sanctuaries anywhere in our maritime region, rising so sharply up from the gulf seas that they are practically unclimbable. I once scaled the easiest part of them but it was a frightening experience, made all the more discomfiting by the ease with which hundreds of birds rode the air, screaming at my presence as I tried to get handholds on rocks often slippery with guano.

But because they are vertical and so heavily populated, the cliffs eventually exercise a mildly hypnotic effect on the human watcher. A friend of mine once spent days there photographing the birds and he was shaken by the experience. "It *is* hypnotic," he said later. "You watch those creatures endlessly flinging themselves away into open space and after a while the thought keeps recurring that you might be able to do the same thing yourself. Just spread your arms out and . . ."

The fascination of the cliffs is enhanced by the diversity of their bird life. The birds occupy them in layers—gannets, kittiwakes, murres, razorbills—so there is almost never a moment when there is no activity.

I have been in a boat at the foot of the cliffs and seen a sudden bolt of murres hurtling away from their place of refuge in a case or indentation high in the cliffs. They stream away, several hundred of them, until their refuge is empty. They stay together half a mile beyond the island, then wheel around with characteristic murre wariness to look back at the island and check to see what has been the threat.

The murres have their individual ways of measuring danger. The kittiwakes do not rise with their characteristic rasping cries in response to the alarm of the murres. The gannets do not move either. Perhaps the other birds remain indifferent because they are so much in the majority. The kittiwakes occupy the cliffs by the thousands and so these small gulls provide an almost constant musical counterpoint to the quieter and less flamboyant gannets and murres. Their frequent blossoming flights away from the cliffs, their cries, intermingling like the threads of a brightly colored cloth, flutter along the walls of the cliffs.

By their sheer massiveness, the cliffs eventually become more than hypnotic; they overpower. The ledges where the birds cluster are only inches wide in places, and although these ledges are dominated by kittiwakes, many gannets are there too. If you wait long enough beneath the cliffs, you see a constant attrition of life. In the silence of midday, when many of the birds are away hunting, a solitary egg silently falls to splat into oblivion at your feet. A small, unidentified chick tumbles down, its piping cries silenced as its body hits the cliff rocks and goes bouncing into the water. It is all rather unearthly and disturbing.

The best time to watch the Bonaventure cliffs—and this applies to all the coastal bird islands—is in the early morning, late afternoon, and early evening. In the morning, the birds are preparing for long-range expeditions to distant fishing grounds, some of them more than a hundred miles away. They fire themselves from the cliffs singly and in small groups. They go arrow straight, north, south, or east. They seem to know exactly where the fishing lies. I have often asked myself whether these early fliers are pathfinders, possessors of some special fishing knowledge, or whether they are accidentally lucky fishermen. Always, though, there is a thickening of birds flying in one direction. It is seductive to believe that the pathfinders are followed by the less adventurous, less knowledgeable birds. Then begins an almost continuous back-and-forth stream of gannets, aimed along a narrow corridor leading toward their fishing grounds for the day.

Bonaventure is the place for the most dramatic view of the dawn. I am surrounded, even immersed in wild life. Fifteen years ago, it was possible to be there without tourists or bird watchers, and it was possible to experience a marvelous sense of freedom as the dawn unfolded its spectacles in sequence. On clear mornings, the theatrical quality of the view is unmistakable. Some talented director has arranged all this. The birds crouch down in the early light, murmuring soft calls to each other. Odd birds pass silently overhead. Then, along almost the full width of the horizon, cut sharp as a knife slice, a band of color appears, a brush stroke of pallid rose, silent and brooding. The color is restless. It rises quickly, replaced by deep red, the color of dying coals. The sun is down there somewhere and it announces itself with an extravagant parade of bands of color leaping up from the horizon. Then its tip appears and I can almost imagine tongues of flame thrown upward. Clouds of kittiwakes rise to greet the sun with a mass dance. Then up go the gannets, silent at first, and then gargling harsh cries, followed by murres streaming away downward from the cliffs. Gulls from the other side of the island begin their prowling flights along the cliffs.

Such moments, alas, are rare. Other people want to see the dawn too, and they have equal rights. The sunrise may be magnificent but behind you, in these more crowded wilderness days, approaching through the island's spruces, comes the grinding roar of an all-terrain vehicle bringing its load of tourists to see the sights. The price of conservation, you may have to remind yourself, is the interest of human beings in it.

III

Moving from island to island is like traveling from one foreign city to another, from one country to the next. Bird Rock, situated almost in the dead center of the Gulf of St. Lawrence, is Bonaventure's nearest relative and is an even bigger gannetry. But by an odd trick of fate, although it is one of the most perfect refuges of all for seabirds, with steep cliffs encircling it, the Magdalen Islands' fishermen pirated it so thoroughly for codfish bait that its populations are still recovering from the disaster. Here, the atmosphere is harsh, austere, even repellent on overcast days. No touch of green illumines the scene, just stark stone cliffs washed with white guano and set against the constant uproar of the gannets massed so thickly they look like a white mantle covering the top of the island rock.

Almost equally stark, but totally invulnerable to the works of man, is the gannetry at Cape St. Mary's, at the southwestern tip of the Avalon Peninsula of Newfoundland. There is no way for either man or beast to climb its vertical walls. The gannetry sits on top of what is really a stone skyscraper extension of the mainland, a scant few hundred feet from the mainland cliffs. It is possible to stand on the cliffs of the mainland, if you have the energy to walk a dozen miles from the nearest village, and look down on this small but utterly secure congregation of birds. This place has its own atmosphere, not stark or unearthly, but touched with the bizarre. The towering rock looks as if an architect had designed it solely as a bird refuge, then arranged for the cliffs to fling gannet cries back and forth with ventriloquial effect to give the place a strange musical background.

Scarcely one hundred miles north and west, Gull Island, off Witless Bay along the eastern coast of Newfoundland, is oddly quiet and serene by contrast. The island is spruce clad, densely massed with undergrowth, and almost impossible to explore systematically or easily. A few puffins and gulls have occupied some of its bare extremities, but this is the island city of the legendary Mother Carey's chickens, or more prosaically, the Leach's petrels. It is an island of the night, and only comes alive long after the sun has dropped behind the Avalon Peninsula of Newfoundland.

Here, particularly on foggy nights, the arrival of the petrels from the open sea occurs between nine thirty and eleven and creates another kind of uproar. But this one is sweetly melodious, made up of the yodeling cries of petrels dashing back and forth through the spruce tops, dropping down through the mist-dripping branches, struggling through the long grass to reach a single burrow where they must find and relieve their mate from his or her duties of incubation.

While the cries come out of the black air above, the ground itself is throbbing with the crooning sounds of the petrels inside the burrow, cries that seem either to be inviting the other bird down to join them, or to be the sounds of two petrels finally united after the traditional three- or four-day absence away hunting.

Every island is a study in the unique. Great Island, a few miles south of Gull Island, is the main metropolis of puffins along the northeastern coastline. When I first climbed its rock shores—there is only one landing place for a man on the entire island—I was exhausted before I had been on the island for an hour. Several hundred thousand birds have occupied this high-cliffed, deeply earthed island and there is hardly a square foot of it that they, the puffins, have not dug out for their burrows. In places, every footstep forward sent me plunging face down as my feet dropped into collapsed burrowings. Despite their numbers, the puffins here give the human watcher none of the exuberance, uproar, display, mystery, or excitement that infuses the other islands. Instead, Great Island is rather dour, a workmanlike place where the silent puffins come and go according to their mysterious and unannounced schedules.

One morning at ten o'clock in the breeding season, I watched all the uplands and cliff edges of the island dotted with the white chests of scores of thousands of silent birds. Offshore, other thousands rose in broadly spaced rafts of birds, equally silent. It was all very chilling, a bit like walking the darkened streets of a totalitarian country under curfew. Then, all at once, the birds disappeared. Those on the island retreated into their burrows. The offshore rafts peeled away, section by section, and disappeared toward the gray horizon.

The function of the island is to provide sanctuary, and therefore the farther offshore it is placed would seem to connote the greatest degree of safety. But this has never been so. The islands are sanctuaries only if they can never be reached by any predator, but the islands close to the mainland have been visited by swimming bobcats, cougars, foxes, even wolves, and thus are made periodically vulnerable. Islands far offshore were, in older times, regularly visited by eagles and falcons, owls and hawks.

All the islands were raided by Indians who prized not only the seabird eggs but also the plumes of the adults. Their flesh could be dried and kept over the winter. Usually, the Indians—and the white men after them—camped on the islands during the breeding season, and systematically robbed nests, but always leaving one egg in each nest so that the bird would attempt to expand her clutch by laying more eggs. On Kent Island, for both Indians and whites, the egg and flesh hunting was a gala occasion when hunting and pleasure were combined in the first fine days after the long maritime winter. At Funk Island, off Newfoundland's coast, the Beothuk Indians used the island as a major source of food and invariably reached it under the cover of thick fog, to the bafflement of white fishermen who had trouble finding the tiny rock island in clear weather. But of all the island sanctuaries, only Cape St. Mary's can claim perfect invulnerability from man.

IV

Finally, one island stands beyond all the others for its unique and repellent atmosphere. This is Funk Island, one of the great natural history wonders on earth, scarcely two hundred yards of rock densely packed with more than a million murres and thousands of gannets, puffins, kittiwakes, and other seabirds. It is, as one visitor once commented, "an astonishment to observe, a horror to contemplate."

Here, in my view at least, is expressed all the exuberance and will to survive that is personified in seabirds. It is a place of almost continuous uproar since the murres cry to one another constantly. The screaming voices of the young remain a background to the major sound which is like a Niagaran surf continually breaking.

The noise is combined with the endless circling of birds over the island, scores of thousands of hurtling bodies whistling overhead, more thousands arriving or leaving the island. All this is part of yet another combination: the manifold smells of bird guano, rotting bodies, broken, addled eggs, stagnant, filth-filled waters, the whole assailing the senses simultaneously and leaving strong-stomached· observers weak with the shock of it all.

Funk Island lies practically in the middle of the Labrador current and is thus just about the most isolated—certainly the bleakest—of all the islands where the seabirds find refuge. Its isolation and its bleakness, combined with the extraordinary noise and smell, have convinced many local fishermen that it is impossible to remain on the island for more than a few days without going insane. I have spent many days on the island, hopefully remaining sane, but sobered after each visit by a surprising disorientation of the senses which persisted for several days after leaving. In that environment, the human watcher has a chance to measure the vast gap that exists between him and the wild things he seeks to observe so closely. But few men ever reach Funk Island and perhaps that is just as well.

THREE: THE OUTER WORLD

I

The world of the seabird is a series of truths which leads gradually to the center of the creature's being. Long before we begin to look at the creatures themselves, we must know a great deal more about the "outside world" they occupy before they come ashore. As a traveler on many of the world's seas and oceans, I have come to understand that the first truth of the seabirds' world is that it is so plastic. No land bird has to contend with such ferocious opposites to survive. Watching the seabirds on our feeble legs and in fragile boats, we are confined to that narrow belt of territory where the birds come close inshore, but their world—their real world—is the entire ocean.

The Atlantic is the second largest ocean on earth. Its average depth is around two miles, its width about thirty-five hundred miles, its length, nine thousand. The seabirds thus skim the surface of a world almost too immense to imagine: thirty-three million square miles of water, seventy-five million cubic miles of a three-dimensional world crammed with an indescribable diversity of life.

We stand on the shore and dumbly watch the arrival of the seabirds who, set against the size of their world, are the sublime end products of a process of unimaginable scope and enormous length in time and distance.

The sun is the great implementer in bringing these creatures ashore. It shines through the upper levels of the water, touching the gases dissolved into it; the oxygen and the carbon dioxide combined with the phosphates and the nitrates, the millions of tons of mineral salts being washed steadily from the land masses of America, Europe, Africa, and the Arctic.

It enlivens what one man has described as a heaving soup of life, and that soup is the home of the plants which start the process that makes the seabird possible. The plants need the sunlight and the salts of the earth. They are a world of their own in miniature, hunted by animals as microscopically small as they are themselves. Together, they form the plankton of the Atlantic. At this genesis point of the seabird, there exist plants and animals in such numbers that it is impossible to talk about billions or trillions. No machine can count them and no man exists with the knowledge or patience to completely comprehend them. Above and beyond them begins the animal world of the fish and the marine mammal which leads eventually to the seabird.

The plankton, a helpless nation of drifters in currents and storms, dying in immeasurable numbers, proliferating in stunning comebacks, are a backdrop to the seabird's world. They dramatize the seabird's superb ability to master this astonishingly plastic environment. All is flux and change in the sea but the seabird has developed an endless and ingenious variety of adaptations that enables him to match the changing conditions and survive.

Survival is no predictable and static thing. Some of the sea creatures have already made exceptionally fast changes of behavior in their efforts to save themselves. Some, like the herring gull, have actually speeded up the normally slow process of evolution to cope with changing conditions. Others, like the flightless great auk, remained locked into changeless modes and so died out.

The herring gull, a bird of beach, foreshore, and estuary, literally took to the trees when danger threatened him, and even nested there in a desperate effort to survive. He proved himself to be an opportunist who showed, in incredibly speeded-up form, how evolution works. Other seabirds show this less dramatically, but each indicates by behavior, form, or placement some clues to its origins.

The murres came from a common ancestor to diverge into two species in geographic isolation. The thick-billed murres probably evolved in northern Siberian waters where, in the tremendous cold, they became one of the toughest and most cold-resistant birds on earth. There, where there was practically no escape from winter ice, the birds either had to adapt or die out.

The common murres, though, probably evolved around the Bering Sea. There, they could always escape south into warmer waters. But over thousands of years of climate changes and of many adaptations, both the species extended their ranges. The thick-billed murres came out of the cold, as it were. They moved around the pole south toward warmer waters. The common murres gradually moved north. As the thick-billed birds colonized practically all of the edge of the ice around the Arctic, they were joined by the common murres who so well intermingled with them that now they have become practically indistinguishable from each other, a single race of creatures in appearance. But they have kept their race memory. They did not, and do not, interbreed.

The petrels, who belong to a great order of birds that includes the albatrosses and the shearwaters, probably came out of an evolution territory of the South Atlantic, while the gannets probably spread from their development grounds in the waters around Southeast Asia and Australia and New Zealand. The gulls, however, are perhaps the only creatures to claim the Arctic as the territory from which they spread all over the rest of the world. Toughened in the northern cold, they eventually broke up into more than forty species, and, of these, the herring gull is one of the most successful. We may think of his Arctic origins when we see him flying warily around the edge of a tern colony and reflect that the terns are probably originally birds of the waters of the Indian Ocean.

Origins, speciations, movements are all speculative, of course, but the changes that seabirds have gone through to reach this maritime world show a dynamic harmonizing of animal and environment, a tiny part of which we may understand, although we have no idea at all just how long or how difficult this process has been.

II

The birds coming ashore now have evolved very little within the Atlantic itself. They are creatures of quite another world which we can only guess at. It is as though they are guests here, recently arrived, perhaps because the Atlantic is a comparatively "new" ocean. One geological theory has it that the Atlantic was created by the drifting apart of the continents. As it opened up, it was colonized from other geographies. This allowed the petrels and terns (and pelicanlike birds from the Indian Ocean), the gulls, the auks, and others to move gradually into this new territory.

The process was slow but now is speeding up because of man's presence. Man has been a godsend for many of the gulls, with his offal dumped almost everywhere and his discharging of sewage directly into the sea. These works have put the herring gull into a population explosion and apparently are bringing down the more wary black-backed gull from his northern home. The opportunist gulls are omniverous for the most part, and adaptable, and so they are the first to respond to the effects of man's presence.

Most dramatic of all, the gull-like fulmar—who is actually related to shearwaters and petrels, not gulls—is in the middle of one of the greatest population revolutions of any bird anywhere. In the eastern Atlantic fulmars have swarmed in competition for rubbish discharged from the thousands of trawlers operating constantly there. But they look like gulls and act like them.

III

Some seabirds flourish but others suffer staggering defeats in the turbulent world of the sea and its shores. Small changes in temperature may be critical. They can bring fish within the range of the seabirds, or remove them. Great armies of brant geese once gathered in the inlets off Grand Manan but were practically wiped out in the 1930s when the eelgrass, their favorite food during migration, was destroyed by a virus disease.

But the eelgrass made its own adaptations and the brant came back.

In April, I see them collecting at Grand Manan, group after group of them leaping out of the water, circling widely and crying out. Then suddenly, the quality of their voices changes and they form up into a series of V's, and turn away toward their sub-Arctic breeding grounds.

Each seabird accurately reflects the precision of this long process of adaptation. When the Arctic or common terns take off from low rock islands and head offshore to hunt, their bodies are light, their wings delicate; they are perfect miniature flying machines designed to reach great distances with minimum consumption of energy. They are hunters at the surface of the sea, and the lightness and fleetness of their bodies forever prevents them from penetrating the water any deeper than a few inches.

In contrast are the razorbills, standing on kelp-clothed rocks, short and squat bodied, wings added as constructional afterthoughts when the designer understood that this craft had to fly as well as swim. We watch them on Machias Seal or along the Scotian shore, launching themselves from rocks with necks bowed down gracefully and bodies arched while they let themselves swoop down fully twenty feet to pick up speed and then drive smoothly offshore. There is no lightness or grace here, merely the simplicity of an efficient flying machine using as little energy as possible to get the body from place to place.

The razorbills resemble all the auks in appearance, but there are mere thousands of razorbills whereas there are millions of murres and puffins. Some tiny differential along the evolutionary path held them back while the others blossomed into great nations. Perhaps they were common once and some change in the shorelines eliminated their traditional nesting places. Perhaps they simply could not compete against the more aggressive hunting of the murres and puffins. Or perhaps they lacked that immeasurable quality of determination—which the ornithologist might call the dynamic—which would have ensured that kind of success.

Once, I remember being about twenty feet underwater among a large school of launce, a small northern fish, when a hunting pack of murres came down through the dusky water in pursuit of them. Like all the auks, the murres work their wings to "fly" underwater and use their feet merely as rudders. But that was not the point of this experience. It was the darting, lean *determination* of the hunting birds that was impressive. They were not simply masters of this water world, they were triumphant in it in a way that impressed me more than when I had seen swimming razorbills.

Last of all, the razorbill most closely resembles the great auk, so perhaps he shares that extinct bird's inflexibility of temperament. Unable to adapt, he remains a vestige of another age.

IV

The sharpest contrast to the razorbill is the ubiquitous herring gull who does not seem to have any special skills, any special reasons for his astonishing success. He has neither speed nor the talent for underwater swimming, neither great endurance nor a ferocious disposition. Instead, he is the generalist who does a little bit of everything passing well. Perhaps his greatest talent is his omniverous gut which can ingest almost anything. There he is, rising and falling over an asphalt road and dropping shellfish. There he is, gorging on blueberries in the highlands of New Brunswick. There he is, at the foreshore, tugging away at the body of a dead seal or a stranded fish. There he is, dropping with delight into masses of swarming herring. There he is, chasing young rabbits. If he makes his kill, he can swallow the animal whole, cramming his great maw to its capacity.

The gulls appear before the human watcher as separate studies in the process of change. The herring gull is expanding in all directions in his exuberant exploitation of new opportunities. He can stand man's presence, even welcome it. But the glaucous gull, beautiful, pale plumaged, which once bred in Newfoundland, has not found man's arrival agreeable. Always an Arctic gull, breeding from Labrador up into the high Arctic, he is retreating as far away from man as possible.

Two other gulls, the Sabine's and the ivory, have long since selected the far north as their territory. They are rarely seen within the self-imposed limits of our watching area. The ivory gull is the more extraordinary of the two. He is the antithesis of the herring gull who is so catholic in his choice of territory that he is found from Greenland to the Gulf of Mexico. The ivory does not breed south of the Arctic

Circle, and he nests as far north as he can find land. But, like all gulls, he is adaptable, and may come briefly south in late winter as he follows the great migration of harp seals into the Gulf of St. Lawrence to whelp. The ivory is their scavenging attendant and when their whelping is done, he returns north.

Because the seabird is so precisely adapted to the sea, he is wary of land. Every great breeding congregation is a study in how to deal with the dangers of land. Once, when we were on Machias Seal, the terns abruptly erupted into one of their panic, or dread, flights. At one instant, the entire colony became silent, every bird swooping down within two or three feet of the ground, and then, in a mass of interweaving bodies, exploding away from the land mass and out to sea as fast as they could go. The motion was so unexpected that we looked around for some dreaded predator. But on all sides of the clear blue sky the air was empty.

This was probably some response to an ancient racial memory of a predator long since disappeared from the territory of the terns. The massed movement of the birds, the speed of their escape, the weaving of their bodies were obviously designed to confuse and mislead the enemy.

Even more dramatic is the arrival of some real danger at a gannet colony or a murre bazaar. An eagle flying leisurely past the cliffs at Bonaventure Island causes such an explosion of voices and flailing wings that it is like a bomb exploding. The gannets climb like fighter planes in their many thousands. The scramble is a sharp lesson in collective security. The eagle understands and moves on as fast as is gracefully possible.

The great congregations of breeding birds are studies in race memories. The distant appearance of a jaeger or a low-flying falcon usually causes immediate panic at a gullery. The blossoming flight of birds is the same kind of explosion as the gannets staged. It warns the intruder of their unity of purpose in defense of the gullery, even though the birds are terrified.

What is impressive is how distantly the gulls recognize the intruder, when he may be nothing but an indistinct blur of movement in the mist or running against a gray wave. What miraculous powers of perception do these birds possess?

Unfortunately for the humanistic watcher, along comes the scientist, with his behavioral bag of tricks, and reveals the miracle as something else. He catches and stains some gulls black and releases them near nesting birds. Panic. He cuts out cardboard or wooden outlines resembling eagles and jaegers and passes them over nesting seabirds. Panic. So our comprehension of the seabird advances a tiny step. He seems—a reluctant concession this—to be a rather mechanical fellow. Or so the man would have us believe. But you have to ask what would be the scientist's reaction if someone confronted him on a dark street with a wooden cutout of a robber armed with a wooden knife.

V

In their land-bound period, the seabirds act in unison not only in response to danger but also to stimulate themselves to common activity. They respond to group leaders by copying them. Dominant herring gulls have the capacity, by displaying excitement, to infect birds all around them. They can set half a thousand gulls to screaming and flying upward for no apparent reason. One bird will imitate another one preening; a third and fourth will follow them, and then fifty or sixty copy the act. These, you say, are comradely, gregarious birds until you encounter a solitary gull twenty miles offshore in midwinter. Gregarious?

Great congregations of seabirds communally stimulate their emotions during the prebreeding period. This apparently coordinates their hormonal development so that they will all be ready to breed at roughly the same time. There is survival value in this. Too many eggs at once for the nest raiders to destroy.

I see murres rising buoyantly, like ascending butterflies, then coming down on softly fluttering wings, like black-and-white parachutists falling to land on water and rock. From high cliffs, I see puffins and murres chasing each other in wild submarine flights and the effect is quite incredibly beautiful and moving. I understand, in the rational part of my mind, that this behavior has a scientific reason. But I prefer to see it all as paradox and mystery, an excitement and an ecstasy of creatures transported momentarily from the hard realities of life at sea.

These creatures do not have "feelings" we are told. They respond to everything mechanically. I can believe this when I see a female herring gull absent herself from her nest for a few moments and watch a nesting neighbor peck at one of her eggs. When the herring gull returns, she calmly eats her own pecked egg. Then she sits down and incubates the remaining egg—or perhaps she will eat it. Mechanical response.

But then, even allowing for nineteenth-century romanticism, John James Audubon once saw a male puffin desperately trying to lift out of the water with his beak the body of his recently shot mate. His efforts were so frenzied and pathetic that Audubon was deeply touched. Twentieth century man can stand, presumably detached, and consider what the purpose was of *that* mechanical response.

VI

The writer can play around with his words, conjecture all he likes, and if he is skillful, he can prove or disprove anything. But the cool eye of the camera is something else. Les Line is there, hunched over for hours in search of that one moment of truth that the pen can never quite catch. He cannot live long enough to get all the pictures. He is not there when the young gull, wary and helpless in the reeds, his broken wing dangling from the blow of an unexpectedly high wave, wanders hopelessly. But he is there to record a great and graceful gannet skewered on a sharp branch. And he sees the razorbill coming in to land, catches him for one frozen second against his blue background of sea, an image of the impossible since his short, thick body is practically upright, like a feathered sausage, and his protruding wings are demonstrably incapable either of stopping him or keeping him aloft.

In the final moments of landing, with his feet splayed down like the flaps of an airplane and his wings working overtime, we watch him and laugh. Not only is it impossible for him to fly; it seems suicidal for him to attempt to land.

Yet the auks have mastered the sea and their brief encounter with the land, and have made it their own. Cameraman and writer stand there and watch the birds in action. At one moment, they are laughing, but the next moment they are dumb and sobered by a feeling of underlying tragedy and pathos.

FOUR: THE QUEST FOR SURVIVAL

I

As I watch seabirds coming in to land, I am reminded less of the millions of new lives about to be created than I am of the struggle that has taken place to reach these breeding havens. At least the island is a shelter. The sea is not. To survive and reach the island at all, the seabird must be master of his plastic, hostile, contrary world.

It is common during storms to see petrels darting along the troughs of waves, pausing every now and then to feed. There, they may be joined by rapidly flying murres who also use the lea of the wave for protection. Standing in my fragile boat which rises and falls in the great waves, I can admire this trick because I am leaning dangerously into the awesome power of the wind. Occasionally, I have seen such birds unwisely rise to the crests of spuming waves, only to be whipped away in a second in the grip of the wind.

Sometimes, far out to sea in a fishing boat, I have heard the crash of bodies hitting the superstructure, or the twang of stays and radio wires as helpless birds smashed into them. Once, when I was sitting in the warmth of the main cabin of a large fishing boat, a pair of murres struck the cabin door with such impact that they burst its flimsy catch and landed sprawling on our supper table. The blow would have killed ordinary birds but the murres kicked all the dishes off the table, bounced from wall to ceiling and dived under bunks before we could catch them and throw them back into the strength of the storm. It was an odd feeling, knowing they were more at home out there than in the relative calm of our cabin.

The sea offers no sinecures. Occasionally, a gale may abruptly change its direction ninety degrees. The waves, of course, are still possessed by the impetus of hundreds of miles of buildup and they cannot change direction. Now, the wind is sweeping along the troughs. There is no shelter, and the wind funnels along the troughs. Petrels, murres, and many other kinds of seabirds are swept away. If there is a mass of land in the path of the wind, they will be driven ashore. Then there will be what ornithologists descriptively call a "wreck."

These wrecks reveal a tiny part of the inner life of the seabird. A wreck occurs when all the resources of the seabird have become exhausted and he is a pure victim of the sea. I remember once being out on the ice pack in the Gulf of St. Lawrence during a spring blizzard which had gathered thousands of seabirds from the open water along the shores of southern Newfoundland and had pushed them into an unbroken world of ice. The birds, dovekies and murres, were in a doubly hostile environment, without shelter, where any attempt to land meant the high risk of mortal injury or crippling.

Some murres, desperately trying to fly diagonally against the wind and snow, lost control. They crashed into the ice and cartwheeled like spinning marionettes. Others chose to fly with the wind, but their strength exhausted, they crashed into upended ice floes and were killed. I found small groups of murres and dovekies huddled together in pathetic groups in the lea of ice hummocks, birds so beaten that I could pick them up. They lay in my hands without struggling.

II

It is easy to imagine seabird disaster in winter, but the sea is impartial and hands out disasters any month in the year. Summer storms, although rare, usually strike with shocking suddenness. They drive offshore fishing birds hundreds of miles from their islands, or kill them against the shores of their own breeding places. Almost the entire maritime region we are watching is the focus of two opposing weather systems which create a great meteorological meat grinder which may stretch from Greenland to the Gulf of St. Lawrence. It is composed of a southern system rotating counterclockwise, colliding with a northern system rotating clockwise. The meshing gears of the two systems can ram gales due west across the maritime region and thence, inland.

These gales have great force and may blow uninterruptedly for days. Seabirds riding out such a storm well offshore are tested to see if their strength can match that of the meat grinder. If they weaken before the storm does, they are forced to ride with it, creating the ingredients of a wreck. Once, thousands of murres wintering in the Gulf of St. Lawrence and elsewhere found themselves caught in such a meat grinder and were swept west into the narrowing funnel of the St. Lawrence river estuary. They lacked sea room in which to maneuver and had long since lost the strength to fly against the wind. They were driven quickly over land where, disoriented even more, they were smashed all along a westward course stretching to Montreal and up the St. Lawrence to Toronto and into the Great Lakes region. Some of these birds, which I must assume were more panic-stricken than exhausted, even reached Indiana.

I have no doubt that in such wrecks psychology is involved. The murres are wrecked, but the puffins are not. While the puffins are stoically riding out the storm on the surface of the waters, the murres are in panicky flight and being swept away overhead. The reason for this difference in behavior, I like to assume, is the same reason that sends the murres joyously aloft at mating time while the puffins stay soberly and silently afloat.

Two birdmen, Peter Freuchen and Finn Salomonsen, once noticed that thousands of murres in west Greenland became panicky in December and January when the fiords of the island froze and they could not find open water. Here, the psychology of panic became strong. "They keep flying around in flocks searching for open water," the two men wrote. "And then eventually fall down on the ice, exhausted or stricken with panic at not being able to find water. Sometimes they stray over the land, where they soon succumb and are found dead or dying, often far from the sea."

The adaptation of seabirds to their world is ingenious enough, but like that of all other animals it tends to be inflexible. Any sudden variation in the norm is difficult for the creatures to accept. Sometimes the meat grinder may last long enough to sweep birds from the coasts of Greenland and throw its victims ashore all along the maritime strand.

A Quebec hunter of the nineteenth century, Napoléon Comeau, once saw dovekies passing his northern gulf coastline for two weeks, almost without a break, millions of them heading west. Here, too, was the suggestion of panic. The birds had been panicked by some earlier, distant storm that Comeau himself had not witnessed. But once the wreck was begun, there was nothing that could stop it.

Perhaps the worst bird wreck in history involved dovekies and it took a bizarre and unexpected direction. Through some unrecorded conjunction of events, the overwintering dovekies of the Greenland area found themselves caught in a meat grinder type of disaster, but one which spun them off southwest rather than due west. They found themselves driven far south along the Atlantic shore, moving parallel to it for thousands of miles, but as their resistance and will collapsed, they were driven inshore almost along the full length of the coastline.

They came inshore as mute and bizarre victims in totally alien places. Most of these small auks had never even seen men or their works. They dropped down into small New England ponds set in the woods, and were unable to take off because of the surrounding trees. They starved to death. They flew into the doors of open freight cars in New York; the doors were shut and the dovekies were dispatched to certain deaths in the Middle West. They came sweeping into the Carolinas, carried by the universally high winds of the storm, and died in their uncounted hundreds when they crashed into electric light and telephone lines. They were found dead by the hundreds along the beaches of Florida, and some of them, presumably in the same kind of panic that sent murres to Indiana, fetched up along the shores of Cuba.

III

Only a very few of the seabirds' disasters are seen by men, but we do know that they are not critical to their survival as species. Almost all of them are long-lived, a testimony to their toughness and mastery of their world through their special skills.

All of the auks have the supreme capacity to swim and hunt fish underwater, a skill they have gained at the cost of strong flight. This is a sensible evolution since they swim all the time and fight wind storms only occasionally. Less sensible, however, is the apparent stupefaction of dovekies by cold, even though they are northern birds. When the temperature drops low enough in the waters of the Labrador current, they huddle together in small, pathetic rafts of creatures where, like the birds seeking refuge on the ice pack, they may be picked up unresisting from the water by passing fishermen.

Despite these odd anomalies, it remains the toughness of the seabirds that scores the memory. The greater shearwater breeds mainly on Tristan da Cunha, an island in the central section of the South Atlantic, midway between Africa and South America. Between nesting seasons, the greater shearwaters spend about eight months at sea without sighting land. They crisscross the great ocean in flights that may total one hundred thousand miles or more in a year while traveling from about thirty-seven degrees south latitude to sixty degrees north latitude and back. The Arctic tern flights, practically from pole to pole, are even more impressive. But all seabirds cover vast distances in conditions that make it difficult for us to understand how they navigate, how they can so accurately pinpoint remote islands, survive the gales, the cold, the ice.

Survival, for the seabird, depends on being in perfect physical condition. It may be my imagination, but it has always seemed that seabirds *feel* different when handled. Their bodies are more compact, more tightly muscled than landbirds, and their strength is surprising, if they choose to struggle. The first time I picked up a shearwater, caught in a fisherman's hook on the Grand Banks, I thought the long-winged, small-bodied bird would be easy to hold while we got the hook out of his throat. But to my surprise, his body was like a steel ball, his paddle feet, armed with sharp claws, so badly flailed and slashed my hands that I almost dropped him. Before we got control of him, he had ripped a piece of flesh clean out of my hand. And all this damage was done by a bird that looked about as dangerous as a pigeon. Anyone who has picked up a puffin can testify to the effectiveness of the vicelike bite from that heavy beak.

(*continued on page 97*)

THE GULLERY

The herring gull's sharp, inquiring eye watches the human intruder with an awareness and a seeming intelligence possessed by no other seabird. On Kent Island in the Bay of Fundy, the species' North American breeding headquarters, the gull is particularly questioning of visitors because it has so thoroughly made this place its own—surviving generations of egg- and feather-hunters from the mainland. The herring gull has outbred and outlived them all—Indians, farmers, fisherman, hunters—and still preserves one habit developed to outwit man, that of roosting and even nesting in trees. Thus the gull looks down on approaching birdwatchers, scientists, and ordinary tourists who come to see more than 50,000 of its kind in one place. And where they have colonized the spruce forest, they have turned their breeding island into a rolling territory of dead and dying trees and exposures of rock.

To foil marauding man, the herring gull had to perform the inconceivable—to use its paddle feet, adapted for walking sand and mud flats and for swimming, to land and stand in the jagged spruces. Every landing and every takeoff is a study in this difficult adaptation. The revealing camera follows the cautious approach of the gull, its intense inspection of the landing place, the tentative outstretching of one foot to steady itself, and then the chancy catching of one claw of the other foot to complete the landing.

With hunting man now gone, the herring gulls of Kent Island have mostly returned to their old habits of nesting on the ground. But the memory of those earlier days remains in the race, and the approach to the nest, with its pipped eggs and fluffy chicks, is still filled with suspicion.

The gulls of Kent Island have much less to be suspicious about today than do the eider ducks that also nest there. The eiders push through the long grass to lay their eggs near the gulls and even, on odd occasions, to lay them in gull nests. This despite the gulls' appetite for duck eggs and nestlings. At hatching time, the eiderlings must run a gauntlet of these hungry predators in their rush for the relative safety of the surf.

The herring gull dominates the Kent Island gullery, as it does so much of the coastline of northeastern North America, but nesting places at the island's highest end are the property of the great black-backed gull. This is largest of all gulls, tough, rapacious, majestic on land or on wing, a gull of northern climes that is expanding its breeding range southward. Fifty miles southwest of Kent Island, as a gull with a destination in mind would fly, the herring gulls and blackbacks share the turf of Petit Manan Island with a third of their kind, the laughing gull. It is a handsome bird with a black head and lead-gray wings and a musical voice, a laughing *ha-ha-ha* uttered overhead.

The murre himself is so physically tough that I have seen fishermen put three and four barrels of birdshot into passing birds, and watched feathers and blood gouts bursting from their bodies without causing them to swerve from their flight. A Canadian ornithologist, Leslie Tuck, once watched a murre and a peregrine falcon in a furious fight on the slopes of Akpatok Island, in the sub-Arctic. Murre and falcon tumbled down a scree slope, the falcon clenching the murre with both talons. But at the bottom of the slope, the murre struggled so furiously that the falcon eventually let go and flew off. The murre, badly injured, staggered to his feet, and with great difficulty, got into the air himself.

IV

This physical toughness is complemented by the seabirds' feathers. Their feathers are denser and more compact than those of landbirds. This sheath of feathers is, of course, the sole barrier between the seabird and death. A dramatic example of deficient feathering is the cormorant. He has made only a partial adaptation so far to the rigors of marine life. He can be seen in clumsy stances on the shore, with his wings bent away from his body as he tries to dry the plumage as quickly as possible. With his plumage wet, he would sink or be unable to take off, and then would drown.

The care and attention of the feather, therefore, is one of the first duties of the seabird. I have watched herring gulls standing in serried ranks on sand banks spending wholesale hours working their preening beaks from one end of their bodies to the other, flattening, arranging, pulling, and smoothing the feather cover.

One of the prime functions of preening is to spread the secretion of fatty material from the gland in the bird's tail all over the feathers in order to get a waterproof sheath. The oil not only waterproofs but also helps to keep the vanelike structure of each feather securely placed in its correct position. The seabird feather, like all feathers, is interconnected by a series of barbs that keeps each unit locked together in an almost impenetrable, propellerlike vane which enables both flying and swimming.

But the feathers do not perform this function automatically, and it is my impression that as the seabird grows older, he must spend longer each day at work on his plumage if he wants to survive. I once knew an old gull who could have been a score or more years old and he never spent less than two hours every morning preening himself on an old wharf piling post. To see him nibbling and poking, gently chewing and drawing feathers through his beak, helped to give me some insight into the realities of his life; he was the fighter preparing himself for the battle of the day that lay ahead.

V

Survival at sea is based on many imponderables. No creature could possibly guard against all of them. Birds are like human fliers, bound on apparently routine flights, who are led astray by wind, or fog, into faulty navigation that takes them to destruction. Seabirds avoid most of the traps set for them by the sea, but shorebirds or landbirds sometimes give us a dramatic example of the scope of oceanic treachery. In the thirties, a flight of lapwings from central England set out to migrate to Ireland. But their destination was covered by fog and so they overflew it and plunged out into the open Atlantic. Lapwings cannot settle on water, so their flight, to be successful, had to be uninterrupted. Thousands of them made this incredible journey and fetched up against the shores of Greenland, Labrador, Newfoundland, and Nova Scotia. The causes of that disaster remain enigmatic, but its quality, its all-embracing involvement, is the truth of the marine world.

Let us take another instance. It is June, the place Bonaventure Island. In the middle of a great fog with a strong east wind blowing, about twenty jaegers land on the island or circle it. These are birds who have come as much as two thousand miles from their Arctic hunting grounds. Their appearance at Bonaventure indicates some northern disaster.

Or, in the same place, an April snow storm blankets the island and suddenly five thousand fox sparrows are seen from one end of the island to the other scratching in the snow in search of food. The reality of the seabirds' world grips the landbird as well. The mortalities of those attempting to make cross-sea migrations are also a commentary on the lives of the seabirds.

All remains unpredictable, unexpected. Fulmars appear abruptly in the southern Gulf of St. Lawrence. They come out of the mists, circle my boat, and then disappear back into the mist without offering any clue as to why they should be so many thousands of miles from their hunting grounds. Then, days later, I see glaucous gulls stalking the rocks of Bonaventure Island or Bird Rock in the middle of the Gulf, or flying along St. John's Harbor in Newfoundland, and wonder again why these Arctic creatures have come south in the middle of summer when they should be breeding in the north.

There is one certain truth about this world and that is its total uncertainty. No uniformity of winter, no common denomination of storm, no agreement about the duration of sunshine or the length of mists obscuring thousands of square miles of shore and sea alike.

Catastrophe comes out of a pure blue sky or out of a star-studded night as easily as it does from the guts of a howling gale. Once, at the height of the breeding season, a premature hurricane struck into this coastal world. The sea wind was so strong that at Bonaventure not even the powerful gannets could cope with it. Those birds nesting on the tops of the cliffs were luckiest; with the great gusts, magnified to eighty miles an hour by the wind shooting up the cliff faces, they could overfly their nests without colliding with the cliffs. Some of them, however, were already so low in flight that they were swept among stunted spruce growth hundreds of feet back from the cliff top and were impaled, like the victims of a human-type massacre, on the sharp spikes of the spruce branches.

For those birds making their landfall against the sheer walls of the cliffs, their landings had to be absolutely accurate. All that day of the storm, during which time the wind did not diminish, dozens of birds died. They came to the castle walls of the cliffs and smashed into bare rock. Or, just as unlucky, they collided in midair with others while straining to master the turbulence of wind rushing upward. Or they were caught in one-hundred-mile-an-hour gusts which sent them spinning into crevices where they were smashed.

As the winds continued, the waves heightened. Soon, one of these waves, perhaps a legendary "ninth wave," struck up the vertical cliff face more than fifty feet. The wave lifted thousands of tons of water upward and scoured the cliff face like some liquid cleaner. It reached the lower levels of nesting gannets and everything was swept away—adults, eggs, chicks—leaving the cliff bare and dripping.

Within an hour, another ninth wave, but this one much bigger, hurled a solid body of water almost to the tops of the cliffs. The rise of the water was majestic and massive. Thousands of adult gannets could see disaster looming and flung themselves away from the cliffs. Some were lucky and escaped, but others were caught as the wave peaked out, exploded at its crest, and roared backward, breaking inside itself and carrying hundreds of birds down with it.

At dawn of the following morning, with the wind subsided but the sea remaining a white torrent at the foot of the cliffs, the tide receded and revealed hundreds of injured, dying, and dead gannets. One night of the seabird was over.

Catastrophes are not always so dramatic. Days of prolonged rain and cold winds are more subtle disasters. Young herring gulls, only recently hatched, are vulnerable, as are young terns. With the rains falling day after day, the efforts of parents to shield the young from the downfall and the wind become a pathetic study in failure. Quite suddenly, just as the murres become undone, the resistance of the gulls or terns breaks down, and the chicks begin dying. In a really bad mortality, a kind of static wreck this, tens of thousands of youngsters may die.

No less dangerous may be a sharp gale occurring within weeks of the young gulls first achieving independence from their parents. Then, just beginning to acquire confidence in flight, but not realizing how truly callow are their wings, they fall victim to collisions with wave tops, trees, the rigging of vessels, and all kinds of other obstructions. Then, they may be seen in groups, walking up and down the beaches and rocks of the shores, their broken wings dangling uselessly.

The new day dawns and the gray seas tumble white as far as the eye can see. Five hundred miles from shore the black shapes of seabirds speed across the roiling waves. They have survived the night, the snow, predatory fish, the falcons and the eagles, the icing of their feathers, and they have come through to live another day. But they mock our own notions of security and question the real meaning of survival on this earth.

FIVE: SPRING OF THE SEABIRD

I

The emergence from the sea of millions of seabirds and their arrival at the land is the most dramatic event of their year. It occurs at a high point of natural history, a time when the majestic southern migration of millions of harp seals is under way, when great numbers of capelin are preparing to spawn on Newfoundland beaches, when the overwhelming invasion of squid from the depths of the Atlantic is building up in the deep sea. But the seabirds outperform them all.

For many of them, this is not merely their first view of solid earth in months, it is also their first view of land in memory. These are sub-adults making a practice run, as it were, to the breeding colony. Immense reluctance to touch the earth at all characterizes the approach of some birds. The land is not only alien but hostile. Even the herring gull, which is at least half a land bird, is wary about taking over his offshore breeding islands. The herring gulls of the Bay of Fundy, which have made such a great gullery on Kent Island, are one of the earliest of the seabirds to move into the new breeding season, and they have plenty of reason for being suspicious of their island. They have contended with generations of human hunters and eggers, but they are safe there now. The island is protected. Nonetheless, there are dozens of experimental offshore flights to check out the island. Many wary circlings precede any attempt to land. Even when it is time to land, the birds are highly nervous. They come down and scream apprehension or rage, then flutter upward again, only to fall once more without quite getting their feet to the ground. When one bird finally makes it and lands triumphantly, a score of his fellows are encouraged to land and stand in the weak March sunshine, their island safe under their feet.

II

Soon after this, two distinct groups of gannets begin to move up the Bay of Fundy. One of these will occupy Bonaventure Island. The other will turn deeper into the Gulf of St. Lawrence to take over Bird Rock north of the Magdalen Islands. These gannets make the earliest land strikes because the Fundy and Gulf area are a good deal warmer than the other, more exposed, seabird areas.

By mid-March, the murres are beginning to move off the Grand Banks and elsewhere into the coastal areas of Newfoundland. The kittiwake flocks, some numbering scores of thousands, are collecting into convivial groups as they feel the stimulus to breed. Some move westward around the Greenland coast, or filter steadily along a circumpolar course, heading toward the rich feeding grounds of the Labrador current area.

By the end of March, even though ice may still touch the coldest parts of the Newfoundland coast, and into April, the murres, the puffins, and the kittiwakes have landed at a score of island refuges; at Witless Bay, at Baccalieu Island, and on Funk Island. Cape St. Mary's has already been colonized by the murres, the kittiwakes, and the gannets.

At the beginning of April, the petrels have begun to visit Gull Island in Witless Bay. They have settled on Kent Island and on three main islands off Nova Scotia as well as on countless smaller scraps of land in the region. They have occupied the cliffs of Bonaventure and have probably reached as far north as Perroquet Island in the Straits of Belle Isle.

All during this buildup period, this premarital adventure time, there is a quickening atmosphere of excitement and expectation.

Even the gulls who have hugged the coastline during the winter are possessed by the same spirit as the others. They burst into the air periodically for no apparent reason. They are joined each day by migrants from nearly all points of the compass. Some birds come out of the west where they have wintered along the St. Lawrence River or the shorelines of the Great Lakes. Some come south from Newfoundland where, for inexplicable reasons, they had migrated north to spend the winter. Thousands of others come up from the south, from as far away as the Gulf of Mexico, from the rubbish dumps of Boston and New York, from Carolina beaches and Florida's shores. Most of these migrants are probably young birds who, in their first dispersion from their gullery birthplace, were forced to go far afield to find winter territories. But their birthplace brings them back.

At Kent Island, a continual flow of hundreds of birds moves daily into the land to make their individual "capture" of their territorial area. All the time, they seem to reinforce the excitement of the moment with repeated bouts of screaming.

The gannets, on the other hand, waste little ceremony in actually making their landfall. Perhaps, one might say enviously, they have had too much fun just merely migrating. Certainly, they seem to enjoy flying for the pure pleasure of it. As they come up the coast, they spend a lot of their time just soaring and are experts at seeking out cumulus cloud formations where they know there will be updrafts. They dislike land journeys since they cannot take off from land, and cannot even rise from the water if there is no wind. Then they rise thousands of feet until they are out of sight of the watcher on land. They have the choice now of pumping along steadily, as is their custom, or of making a long fast glide to lower heights. But sometimes groups of birds choose to soar above six and seven thousand feet, disappearing into clouds and remaining there for an hour or more, just gliding for the fun of it.

The movements of the gannets to their breeding homes cannot be charted, of course. Random observations do not give a clear picture of the entire thrust of these birds from the Gulf of Mexico and Florida along the full length of the American coast. But I have seen them arriving at Bonaventure. They are almost always in the company of larger groups of birds from which they peel away and head directly for the island. The other birds forge on north to other breeding colonies. Sometimes, the gannets travel in the company of Canada geese and it is a moving sight to see the species separate because the geese customarily migrate at much higher altitudes than the gannets. The great white birds peel away and fall, like fighter-bombers in attack, and approach Bonaventure at tremendous speed. They set down abruptly and without ceremony at the cliff tops.

The murres, however, will have none of this. They are almost as excitable as the gulls, and certainly the land is as dangerous to them. They begin gathering offshore in rafts of several thousand birds even while miles of ice separate them from the islands where they will breed. But the ice and bitter cold of the north do nothing to suppress the excitement. The birds dance on the surface of the water. They trace patterns, circles, ovals, figure eights as they "fly" on the surface, beating their wings and legs clumsily. As they dance, others dive and chase one another underwater so that the watcher may distinctly see them "flying" at three levels—in the air, on the surface, and underwater.

As the murres come nearer and nearer to their moment of truth, which is the land, the excitement intensifies. Towering joy flights develop with the birds sometimes rising high over their Cape St. Mary's cliffs, or above the flanks of Baccalieu, or over brooding Funk Island's impregnable granite bulk.

But this movement is not merely confined to our own territory of watching. It pushes on a thousand miles farther north and it will be almost mid-June, nearly four months after the first murres began landing in Newfoundland refuges, before all the Arctic islands are occupied.

Their exuberance is unique, made all the more so in contrast to the closely related puffins who look like murres, fly like murres, and are auks. But the puffins have dispensed with the joy flights. Their island arrivals have a touch of mystery about them. They appear quite suddenly offshore, their floating rafts half-obscured in late winter mist, and they remain there for hours, unmoving except for the steady rise and fall in the swell. Then, without warning, they all take off and disappear. But they are back again next day and the ceremony, if that is what it is, goes through its enigmatic course again.

Their appearance may lack the drama and excitement of the murres, but they are going through exactly the same motions. They are preparing themselves for landing and they have merely chosen a different way to do it. After ten days or so of these offshore gatherings, the first of them takes off and approaches the island, and here, they display gull-like wariness. For hours, groups of birds circle the island in what seems to be an endless reconnaissance. Gradually, these "inspection" flights become more intimate, and the puffins begin zeroing in on the headland, or the bay, or the high cliffs, or inland hills of grass where their burrows are located. Then they flutter like murres as they come down, rise again, flutter hesitantly, and finally make their landings. These are patient, stolid creatures, I assume, because now they are content to spend hours standing and waiting before making any attempt to enter their burrows and begin the work of spring construction and refurbishing.

By the time the far northern seabirds are emplaced on their Arctic islands, the entire Gulf of St. Lawrence, the shores of Newfoundland, the Bay of Fundy, the Gulf of Maine are working full blast at bringing up a new generation of seabirds.

III

The spring of the seabirds is more than mere courtship and mating. It is a point of vast transformation. The relatively dull-colored creatures are transmuted into something quite amazingly delicate in their behavior. And the puffins grow that extraordinary embellishment to their normally slender beaks that gives them their unique appearance.

The complexity of the courtship and mating process is revealed in many forms, most of them not understood by men. Murres form themselves up into double lines and swim together in a marine corps de ballet as precisely choreographed as anything done by man. All the senses are heightened; a thousand subtle and unseen things govern behavior and the future. There is a reason for every touch of color on a bird's plumage. The yellow-gold marking on the head of the gannet has meaning. The white sides of murres flashing as they spin and dart under the water have meaning. Each species of the auks has different colored mouths, yellow in puffins, bright red in the guillemots, and a kind of garish yellow in the razor-billed auk. In the middle of all their various dances and ceremonialized posturings, the auks open and shut their mouths repeatedly. Secret messages in color are being passed back and forth between them.

Everything is signficant. The sheer press of numbers which seems like chaos to us watching is necessary for metabolic development. There is advantage in having all the birds coming to breeding condition simultaneously. For other birds who do not mass, there is no concert of the breeding effort. The terns trickle into their island sanctuaries over days, or even a week or more, and show no early signs of emotion. They sun themselves along the shores of the various islands, particularly on Machias Seal. Nothing much seems to be happening. Fog rolls in and the foghorn roars. Clear skies reveal a perfection of blues all around. But gradually the excitement mounts and courtship begins. The males dance in front of their prospective mates with puffed-out chests and bills raised. They fly rapidly out to sea and catch small fish, particularly sand eels, and feed them to the females. The art of gift-giving is also the act of courtship.

Unlike the majority of landbirds where the males are identifiably different from the females, all seabirds are dressed in the same raiment, indistinguishable except for slight differences in size. There are even some ornithologists who doubt that one seabird can tell the sex of another until he or she sees the other dancing, or fighting, or displaying the body in some characteristic way.

We can believe that or not, but it is certainly true that the male seabird courts one female and sticks with her throughout the breeding year, sharing guard duty, incubation, and feeding of the young. He is, as one birdman puts it, a model husband. He is so well "married" during this period that the cynical human, remembering that the male has probably spent a rough winter hunting pretty much alone, is hard put to explain how he is able to stay monogamous when he comes ashore and is surrounded by countless thousands of willing brides.

There are some partial explanations for this fidelity. Seabirds generally have the most intricate and extraordinary ceremonies anywhere in the bird world. All the birds preen each other, or rub their bills together, or grip and shake bills, or display their wings in certain attitudes, or contort their bodies in peculiar ways. This ceaseless courtship cements the marriage bond, say the experts, and keeps the family unit inflexibly together. Simultaneously, the ceremonies of the adult birds are watched and copied by the chicks still in the nest so that the entire family becomes united in its behavior.

The ceremonies merge into each other, the chicks copying their parents, the parents seeming to copy the chicks. One of the most common ceremonies of the courtship period is gaping, in which the female seems to revert to being a chick again. The female terns of Machias Seal crouch down, supplicating their mates for food, with their beaks open and their wings shaking. At almost the same time, the female gulls of Kent Island are also begging their mates for food. Meanwhile, the gannets of Bonaventure and Cape St. Mary's stand together at the place where they have made their nest, rear their heads upward and clash their beaks together. On the silent hills of Great Island, puffins appear and with quick deft movements, so reserved they seem designed not to be seen at all, rub their beaks together. These displays, which begin before mating and seem to be solely courtship displays, do not stop after mating but go on throughout the breeding season, after the nest is built, the eggs laid, the nestlings reared to maturity. It has always been my impression, though, that at the beginning of the breeding year, the birds are serious about their displays, but that later, they are more playful.

The ceremonies may be only partially understood after lifetimes of study, but for the layman, they are a perpetual source of surprise and puzzlement as he intuitively senses the multitude of meanings that can surround each activity. The seabirds must solve the territory problem so that each bird, as with the gannets packed together, is just beyond the pecking range of the nearest neighbor. Each species must solve the problem of what to do with the newly arriving youngsters who are ready to breed for the first time, or who are merely to be onlookers for this year at the breeding colony. Usually, they are relegated to the periphery of the group, the most dangerous area, while the most seasoned and experienced adults almost always have their nests in the middle of the congregation, a place earned by them through their succcess and dominance in previous years.

Just watching the nest-building act is a study in ceremony in which there are many unanswered questions. There is much freighting back and forth of nesting material, much of it uselessly since some birds use little or no material in their nests or burrows, and the murres do not build nests at all. The puffins seem to have a memory of nest-building before they began to dig burrows, because they are often seen picking up stones, throwing them down, flying aimlessly with feathers in their beaks (which they do not attempt to add to the burrow nest), or carrying clumps of grass and perhaps dropping them in midair. Many of the terns on Machias Seal feel so secure that they breed on the open ground, without bothering to build nests.

The entire nest-making and nest-sitting act is a dynamic and ever-changing affair. The old birds die off and leave vacant territories in the middle of the congregations, enabling younger birds to move in and take their places. This, in turn, lets the very young get a breeding foothold at the edge of the colony.

But despite the firm bond of male and female, despite the occupation of the same nesting place by the same female year after year, it would be a bold man who would claim that seabirds mate for life, or that territory once earned remains inviolate.

Many of the colonies of seabirds are mixed. Kittiwakes, puffins, murres, gulls, and gannets may all be breeding in the same general area. Courtship and mating is then a time of great tumult. Territory, that vital ingredient in the nesting of any winged creature, becomes critical.

The gulls, which usually occupy the highest ground that they can find, may be constantly harried as they fly along the cliffs where the kittiwakes seem to be in an almost continual state of fighting rage. Along the crowded cliffs of Green Island, off Witless Bay, the fighting is bitter and prolonged. Many of the fighting kittiwakes lock beaks together while they beat each other with their wings and claw desperately with their paddle feet. Sometimes they fall like writhing snowflakes down to the water in such apparent distress that the gulls swoop down. They mistakenly assume that they have seen the fall of crippled, and therefore helpless, birds.

All of this is part of a great canvas of ritualized behavioral rules evolved to ensure that the gullery, ternery, gannetry, and other bazaars of birds operate efficiently and effectively. While the first view of the ceremonies is fascinating, it progressively becomes more baffling. It took me many years of watching to understand that one of my most dearly held convictions about animal behavior is not true. The most aggressive, the most strong, the most ruthless male birds do not always achieve dominance in the group or over the disputed territories.

I have always been impressed by the rarity of really vicious fighting and fascinated by the number of threats, instead of fighting, that control behavior. To watch two gulls facing each other, usually in some dispute over territory, standing absolutely still but with their necks slightly elongated, is to see the gull equivalent of two men with their fists up and ready to punch. But the gulls do not have to fight, and in some mysterious way, the "fight" is often resolved when one of the gulls shortens his neck slightly. He has "submitted" and he may walk off, leaving the victor behind. On Kent Island, during the early breeding season, when literally thousands of gulls are working out their manifold territorial and mating problems, I have sat fascinated for hours watching gulls facing each other, ripping up beaksful of grass, just as though they were about to begin building nests. But the grass ceremony is the equivalent of the bull pawing the ground. It is *instead* of fighting.

Real aggression is common enough, of course, and fighting seabirds can put on shows of violence that are pretty impressive. A gull grabs another's wing and throws him over a cliff. Two murres lock together in a flurry of legs and wings and roll down rocks into the sea. But mostly, because fighting is nonproductive, these devices are aimed at suppressing, redirecting, or overcoming the aggression and channeling it into more useful, productive results. These, paraded before the human watcher, are object lessons about behavior generally. It is no wonder that the animal behaviorists think they have something to tell the world. They may be right, but I suspect, for the rules to work, that you have to buy the whole life package, and that is not so credible.

Aggression, that word made malignant in human society, is no simple act. The supremely aggressive individual male bird, such as a herring gull, may actually *reduce* his chances of mating successfully by not being able to control his fighting tendencies. After subduing all his male rivals, he may then turn and attack the love object herself, the female. The female's influence on him then must be dominant. She must modify his aggressive behavior productively. This is just one way—and there must be countless other ways we cannot recognize —that a kind of internal cosmos is achieved out of external chaos.

IV

Watching the breeding birds is to witness a corner of a great hidden picture. Just the preservation of the egg is an enduring problem. Almost all seabird colonies have their predatorial populations of egg eaters. The herring gulls, skuas, fulmars, terns, and others which build their nests on open ground with practically no cover face the problem of the egg being blown or dislodged from the nest area.

The herring gull uses her beak to try to roll back the egg over the rim of the nest. The tern attempts (not always successfully) to wriggle her body so as to move her nest egg to join the dislodged egg.

But for those birds nesting on cliff faces, no egg retrieval is possible. The slightest mistake and the egg is lost forever. The kittiwake partially solves the problem by building a mounded nest with a deep basin. The murres, which do not build nests at all but lay their eggs on bare rock, produce a long, oval-shaped egg with one end much narrower than the other. Thus, when the egg rolls, it tends to turn in a tight semicircle and does not always go over the edge of the cliff. The gannets build high, deep-dished mounds and defend the nest area ferociously. The eider ducks and some of the gulls take to the dense grass cover where it is difficult for anything to find their nests, and then they cover the nest in their brief absences with a beautifully knit blanket of their own down.

But to me, at least, the greatest puzzle of all remains that of recognition. Of course all strange creatures (including human beings, for that matter) tend to look alike to the uninitiated observer, yet a high degree of selective recognition is so great among some seabirds that it far surpasses our capacity to recognize different members of our own kind.

Not only may a herring gull start up from dozing at her nest in the middle of an uproar of cries in which not one single voice can possibly be separated from another, but it is clear that she has responded

(continued on page 145)

THE PUFFINRY

The puffin is an evolutionary joke whose humor reaches the most dedicated bird-haters. Its jaunty stance is humanoid, and its large scarlet, yellow, and blue beak belongs in a tropical jungle. The squat, chunky body is supported by a pair of the most preposterous wings ever appended to any flying bird. Indeed, judged by the slide rule of the aerodynamic engineer, they should make flight impossible. But no one has told this to the puffin; or told it that it is impossible to catch a mouthful of fish, one at a time, without dropping any. So the puffin goes right on being a parody. Yet behind its jauntiness, those pretty markings, that cuteness, there is a creature made of steel who survives on hostile northern shores where pounding waves can shake an island's very foundation.

How a puffin can possibly fly may be debated endlessly, but there can be no disagreement that it flies badly. The stubby wings flail at high speed, the chunky body rocks from side to side, the flared tail and splayed feet are used to get as much bite on the air as possible. Sometimes, in the open sea, puffins crash into waves. They are so tough they bounce into the air, or bob up, unharmed. Occasionally they even collide in midair. But those wings, however absurd for aerial flight, are superb propellers for the puffin's flight underwater in pursuit of fish.

The difficulties of puffin flight are not helped by its choice of breeding places—usually desolate, bleak islands where the wind often rips over bare rock and turf at near hurricane force. Because the puffin is so superbly adapted to the one thing it does well—swimming—it even has difficulty walking on its stone islands, like Machias Seal, clambering up and down rocks, or jumping from boulder to boulder, wings working furiously.

The puffin takes full advantage of wind and wave. If it must fly at sea in high winds, the bird does not take off until it is sitting deep in the trough of a wave, thus escaping the danger of being blown away in those first vulnerable airborne seconds. When landing, the puffin never makes crosswind or downwind approaches. Instead, it will fly the full length of the island, perhaps a mile or more, so that it can curve around and come to its resting place with the wind in its face. Thus a puffin island, like Machias Seal, is a study in the ballet of seabird flight as the birds wheel into the wind and flutter against it, like great clumsy butterflies but buoyant as thistledown. . . .

Slowly the approaching puffin comes down, sometimes hovering motionless when the wind gusts stronger, until the rock that is its destination lies directly ahead and below. Now the puffin's entire body is strained with concentration. Although the bird appears to be in control, it is utterly dependent on the force and direction of the wind. If either fail, the puffin will crash or miss its target entirely. . . .

If there are other puffins on the rock where the incoming bird plans to land, they understand its predicament, and they do not trust its flying skill. They watch apprehensively, crouch down, and if the newcomer makes the expected mistake, there will be a crash and a clot of struggling birds will spill over the edge of the rock. But if the landing is successful, all the puffins will stand straight and, in the eyes of a human observer, seem to be delighted that all went well.

The puffin spends hours meticulously caring for its sleek plumage, facing into the cool sea wind, wings outstretched and shaking, or attentively preening the feathers on its back and drawing the wing feathers through its beak again and again.

How a puffin can catch more than twenty fish and pack them into its beak without dropping any has intrigued observers for centuries. Someone even speculated that the fish became paralyzed by the sight of that large beak coming at them, and were easy to pick up while they lay stunned on the bottom of the sea. In truth, the puffin's sheer speed underwater is one key to its fishing prowess.

More recently, puffin experts have theorized that the bird nips the caught fish, one by one, with the hooked tip of its beak, killing it instantly. As each fish is captured, the puffin uses its tongue to push the others to the back of the beak, where they are wedged between backward-sloping ridges on the roof of its mouth. The delicacy of each movement can hardly be imagined. The puffin's prey—very small herring, sand eels, and others—usually have fragile bodies; the edge of the puffin's beak is as sharp as a knife; and it is flying underwater through hordes of frantically escaping fish. This is one of the minor mysteries of the sea, however it is explained.

[*Overleaf*]
On many of its breeding islands the puffin nests in burrows dug in the soft, shallow turf, and eggs and young are vulnerable to marauding gulls that have recently learned to reach into the holes and snatch the contents. But on Machias Seal, the puffin has the protection of deep clefts in a rock fortress built by glaciers and storms. There the single egg is laid, and when it hatches, the puffin pair will spend weeks bringing beakful after beakful of fish to the puffling. But for the last week of its nest-bound days the youngster is left alone and fasting. Finally, the full-grown puffling will emerge from its hole, usually under cover of darkness, and make its way to the sea.

In sharp distinction to the comic puffin is the sleek, determined-looking razorbill. In flight and agility it appears to be a far more competent bird. Yet the razorbill's population is but a tiny fraction of the puffin's, dozens measured against thousands. Once it may have been more numerous, but it is less gregarious than the puffin and its breeding rate may be slower. The razorbill closely resembles the extinct great auk, except for its smaller size and its ability to fly. Perhaps it, too, is coming to the end of its evolutionary development in a world that has no room for auks.

The global rhythms of their world put most of the life of seabirds beyond the eyes and understanding of man. They have fitted themselves into one of the most hostile environments on Earth and have survived triumphantly. The puffin hovers against the sea wind, and the moon, which creates the tides and moves the fish and changes the currents of the world, rises as one visible friend to seabirds everywhere.

to the call of a bird which has not yet even appeared. He eventually comes into view, and she is waiting for him expectantly. The human watcher must wonder how on earth he signaled his approach when there is such an uproar in the gullery.

The problem of recognition is complicated by the differences that seabirds show in tolerating individual members of their own kind. Some birds seem to be given almost universal tolerance in their movements about a colony. But others can scarcely make any move without being viciously attacked. Individual gulls can recognize other individuals when fishing far offshore. They can also recognize enemies of their own kind whom they will not tolerate near their shore territories. There even seems to be a special language between birds which know each other.

This, in the eyes of skilled observers, may all be obvious enough. But in the huge bazaars of the auks, individual recognition, even territorial possession, seems incomprehensible to the layman and, one suspects, to the expert as well. I have seen a female murre with a fish in her beak, wheel against the early morning sun and come down for a landing at Funk Island. Under her was packed a mass of more than one hundred thousand birds standing shoulder-to-shoulder on nests or near them. She broke her flight with her wings and landed expertly in the one spot where her one chick was waiting for her.

All this is baffling enough. But after I have watched and listened to the massed voices of the murres, with their Niagara-like quality of one, collective voice, I ask myself why such continual uproar? And why does it go on throughout the night? Is it, as some say, a massed voice to repel intruders? Is it the maintenance of a continuous breeding excitement that helps coordinate and harmonize the behavior of all the birds together? But when I sleep for several nights on Funk Island, the great sound all around me, rational explanations become feeble.

If it is indeed communication among a million individuals, one voice communicating with another voice, the screams of the young underlying the growling voices of the adults, what can there be to communicate about so continuously? I always leave Funk Island a good deal less instructed than when I first set foot on it. The scientific literature, much as I respect its integrity, always crumples to rubbish in my mind. I have often chosen to retreat from the islands altogether and seek simpler visions yielding simpler answers. I walk along the jumbled rocks of the shore and see individual guillemots speeding away from their nesting sites hidden deep in the rocks. These birds, like the puffins and murres, are auks too. Their solitary appearance is a contradiction of all the other adaptations of the family. Are they the losers, when only six of them may live along fifty miles of coastline while a million of their relatives subjugate entire oceans? And what decreed their "loss"? For me, the auks leave more questions than they provide answers. They are very old people in the sea, and perhaps their wisdom so far exceeds our own, in our artificial world, that they will always remain incomprehensible.

V

A change of pace in seabird life is provided by a leisurely pursuit of the great blue herons who thrive in the center of the territory we are watching. To reach them usually means a walk through the forest, far from the shore, because they choose impenetrable places to fasten great bulky nests as high as they can. Built-up mystery surrounds the approach to the heronry because you know you are coming to the largest sea-loving birds in the region. They stand higher than the largest eagle and have a wing span almost as wide. There is much less contradiction and confusion here when young herons are in their nests. From high in the trees, the cries of the youngsters can be heard like the ticking of clocks in a shop. The cries speed up mechanically as we approach. These sounds, in conjunction with the thick green forest all around, diffusing the light from above and combining with the thick moss and ferns underfoot, make the heronry a place with a special atmosphere.

But here also is a touch of the pathos that is visible among the young gannets and murres in their attempts to grow. Having chosen such high stations to escape their predators, the herons are unable to help fallen youngsters. They huddle on the forest floor, weak and starving, and eventually die, while the busy life of the heronry, the coming and going of parents feeding their young, continues on unheeding above them.

In a sense, the spring of the seabird is not over until he goes back to sea again and leaves his islands and his cliffs empty once more. The spring is a sustaining motif of assertion and survival which is not really ended until the young birds are out at sea themselves, with or without their parents, and their world turns slowly toward another inevitable spring.

SIX: THE YOUNG SEABIRDS

I

Watching the whole breeding process leaves me with a flood of impressions, from those flaring mating dances of the murres to the noisy occupation of various islands by the herring gulls. One of the most memorable moments is hatching time. If the weather has been equable and mating begun among all the birds simultaneously, then hatching may involve thousands of eggs in one day. I walk among the close-packed nests and actually hear the process beginning. There must be no wind, and it should be early morning or late evening when the cries from the bird colony are not overpowering. Then, on all sides, I hear the hammering, the clicking, the tapping, the movements of hundreds of tiny lives struggling to free themselves from their eggs. I look down and see the speckled eggs with holes broken in their sides, the eggs rocking back and forth with the intensity of creatures trying to escape. I see nests moving with rumpled, downy figures just released from imprisonment.

There is no agreement among the young seabirds as to how best to cope with the early days of escape from the egg. The puffins wisely stay in their burrows until they are almost fully fledged before they appear warily at burrow entrances. The young petrels are never seen for any reason. The gulls and terns and murres leave their nesting areas and wander, some of them quite widely. Young gulls gather together in comradely groups to sun themselves on high sandy or rocky places at the gullery. Young murres gather together in dense black lines, and

I am often baffled to understand how individual mothers can ever recognize individual chicks. The terns scatter, and their mottled plumage blends into the grassy backgrounds on which their parents have nested so that they become practically invisible.

Even at this time, the possibility of panic haunts the young seabird. Young herring gulls, almost ready to fly, are particularly prone to panic. One time, when a small but intensely occupied gullery on top of a steep rock off the coast of Nova Scotia was about ready to release its crop of youngsters to the sea wind, the island rock was visited by some bird watchers. I had already been to the top of the rock and had noticed the extreme concern of the young gulls. I advised the bird watchers not to walk out among the youngsters. Nevertheless, they climbed to make "a cautious reconnaissance."

I stood at the bottom of the rock and watched a heavy sea crashing at my feet and wondered what might happen. The last of the men disappeared over the top of the rock behind me and a few seconds later, panicked young gulls streamed over the edge of the cliff and fell helplessly a hundred feet down to the rocks nearby. Most were killed or crippled, about two hundred birds, a sad note to the comradely gathering of youngsters that I had witnessed a few minutes before.

II

The long lives of seabirds is both a surprise and a confirmation of the world they live in. Their longevity is often related to impressive physical strength but the fragile-looking petrels and the wide-ranging, delicately structured shearwaters also live as long as the "stronger" oceanic birds. This fact is central to all seabirds. Almost the entire process of natural selection is completed when the seabird is young.

From the moment it hatches until the time it reaches adulthood, the young seabird is more vulnerable than almost any other warmblooded animal. Ninety per cent of all the deaths occur in that period. As human watchers, we are fascinated and horror-struck because death is so omnipresent wherever we wander.

The kittiwakes, in a good year, produce so many youngsters in cliffside nests that hundreds of the young and still unfledged birds jump or fall to the rocks or sea below. At first, these accidents arouse the parent kittiwakes to great emotion. But then their concern cools, or appears to, as predators, particularly the larger gulls prowling the cliffs, methodically kill and eat the young victims. But what mysterious process is it that causes such accidents? What determines who shall fall and who shall not? And why do practically no chicks fall when bad weather makes the breeding less productive?

The odd waxings and wanings of death rates remain inexplicable. In the bad mortality years, the rate of death seems almost wanton. In a really large murre colony, such as the one on Funk Island, the wastage of youngsters is appalling. The tiny black creatures cluster together, little more than balls of fluff, and are trampled by the massed numbers of the adults around them. They are knocked into foul green scummy pools by the general press of birds. There, screaming, they either struggle free, or drown. Dead youngsters lie everywhere under briefly hot suns. Abandoned eggs roll in hundreds of thousands into crevices. On hot days, the explosions of rotting eggs is a punctuating background to the screams of tiny murres drowning or falling to their deaths into the sea, into pools, or into holes in the granite rock body of the island.

But why such mortality at all? Why such a wave of death when the great seabird bazaar idea makes so secure a place for all to be reared to maturity? The answer lies, apparently, in the need for the self-regulation of their own numbers. The mortality of the young perhaps is greater today than it was in the days when eagles and gyrfalcons and peregrine falcons regularly visited the colonies, before the white man decimated them. But there are many other reasons and these are buried too deeply in the seabird past to be accessible to us.

Each species has evolved its separate methods of survival for the young, and these means are not always comprehensible to us. Why the young petrels should be abandoned in their burrows in the fall by their parents is a mystery. They are left in burrow darkness while their parents migrate thousands of miles to the southeast. Why, when these nestlings have never seen the outside world and are the most fragile of all the seabirds, must they face the greatest challenge?

There are no answers to such questions. The young petrel, fat from the rich and nutritious oil food that he has been receiving, comes out of the burrow one night, hungry to the point of starvation, gets himself free of the grasses around the burrow, or fights his way upward in a first flight through the overhanging spruces. This nocturnal escape from the island in a first flight, in darkness, for a day-loving bird is the ultimate puzzle. Nobody knows the mortality of young petrels but it is evidently not high. Petrels mature late, breed sparingly, and lay only one egg, but they are long-lived. Perhaps, having so well mastered their world, their self-regulation is to give the youngster an appalling challenge at the beginning of his life.

The young puffins are deserted too, but the abandonment has none of the drama or pathos of the petrel youngster's beginning. They, too, are fat and being totally daylight birds, they eventually come out of their burrows during the hours of light. They look oddly naked because they lack the heavily ornamented beak of breeding adults. They wander down through the grasses of Great Island or across the bare rocks and shingle of Machias Seal or along the foreshore of Funk Island, waiting for the moment when they must take to the sea.

The young gannets are not deserted, although it sometimes appears so. The adults, having fattened them well, begin spending longer and longer periods at sea. The young gannets stay fairly close to their nest mounds at first, but then they begin to gather in small groups, waiting for the signal to leave the island.

The departure of the young seabirds can have great dramatic impact. This is best seen on Funk Island where, in the early fall, the murres begin gathering together in massive groups that can only be called separate armies. The first army advances down the sloping rocks of the island to the shore, youngsters and adults packed tightly together. They pause along the edge of the breaking waves, a dense and noisy black mass of creatures. Then, in an encompassing wave of black, they take to the water and swim offshore. Over ensuing days the other armies follow them, all swimming offshore quickly, ducking and diving as though glad to be free of their island. But at Bonaventure, where the murres nest high, they jump and fall a hundred feet to the sea. It is an enduring myth among fishermen that the female murres, and other cliff-breeding seabirds, carry their youngsters on their backs in that first flight to sea.

The departure of the young gannets is most dramatic on the islands of the high cliffs, the cathedrallike spire of rock at Cape St. Mary's, the towering cliffs of Bonaventure, or the high ground of Baccalieu in Newfoundland. The young gannets seem to need some special signal which will send them off on their first flight. Watching them, it is easy to understand their hesitancy because in the takeoff that confronts them at Bonaventure, they must throw themselves headlong into mid-air, into what looks like a fathomless void, particularly when it is foggy. They display their doubts. They gather at the edge of the cliffs in groups and look down, pausing, then they walk back from the edge as though it is all too much. They behave as if this were an artificial situation, as if they should not have been abandoned to make this first flight. One feels an almost overpowering urge to reassure them, to make them "believe" that their first flight will not, in fact, be the disaster that it sometimes is.

When young seabirds leave their islands, a note of sadness comes into my imagination. Fall is approaching. Each of the young bird species leaves in his different way but none has quite the individuality of the cormorants. Some young seabirds leave reluctantly, others race for the sea. There is nothing, however, quite like the rush of the cormorants from their islands. They are like groups of unruly children. They come down from the crest of their islands, crying at one another, using feet and beaks and wings to clamber over rocks, piling on top of each other as they race for the sea.

Then, when they are all splashing clumsily in the water, they attempt flight. It is odd that they are, after all, a species already ill-adapted to taking off from water. With many wild thrashings of their wings, they get into the air, one by one. Behind them, their islands stand bare as deserts.

The departure of the young eider ducks is a spectacle of the late afternoon and early evening, but it is not the timing that is important. It is the quality of their departure from the islands.

Even when the ducklings have reached the water—and this is a spectacular scene with the red sun flaming the sea as it sinks into the continental land mass beyond—there is no reassurance. The gulls still attack, and the ducklings, diving to escape them, often come up well separated from their mothers whereupon they are immediately seized by the gulls.

All the juvenile seabirds seem to have a special protective capacity to survive the first great crisis of their lives. Like the celebrated jump of the wood ducks from their high nests when, flightless, they must reach the ground in a wild leap, so do nearly all the seabirds take great falls. Young gannets or murres can drop fully a hundred feet, hitting bare rock, and survive. With that adaptive capacity so well developed, their vulnerability to other dangers becomes all the more noticeable.

III

The mortality of the young seabird is the clue to the long lives of the adults. It is hard to imagine, moving from one outwardly idyllic scene to another, with parent seabirds bringing food into their young, that millions must die now so that only the toughest will be required to face the winter. But seabird life is filled with paradox and contradiction, and no creature exemplifies this better than the eider duck.

The eiders nest along practically the full length of the immensely long coastline on both Gulf shores—Maine and St. Lawrence—and along the Nova Scotian and Newfoundland coasts. Wherever they have established themselves, they are accompanied by gulls. The gulls relish both the eggs and the young eider ducklings themselves. The rush of the young eiders for the sea, especially if they must traverse a wide foreshore in the low tides of the Bay of Fundy, is one of the more unforgettable sights of anybody's life if there happens to be a concerted attack of gulls during their rush.

But the odd thing that eventually strikes the watcher is the peculiar relationship that has been worked out between eider and gull. The eggs and the ducklings may be attacked regularly in one area, or on one day, but not in other areas, or during other days. The gulls even seem to deliberately avoid taking eggs or ducklings on certain occasions.

When we visited Green Island in the Gulf of Maine, that scrap of rocky land which can be reached from Petit Manan at low tide on foot, the eiders and the rapacious black-backed gulls were nesting together. There, amid a maze of bird-made tracks leading through the greenery, duck nest stood close to gull nest. Female eiders left their nests and went out to sea while female blackbacks were returning to their nests, often using the same corridors through the greenery. The gulls passed by eiders' nests. Surely they were not fooled by the eiderdown covering the duck had flung over her eggs on departure? But the gulls ignored the nests, walked to their own, and settled down.

Then later, the lagoon in the center of the island was studded with young ducklings strung out behind their mothers and swimming within minutes of leaving their nests. The great gulls passed back and forth overhead without paying any attention to the ducklings. As if in response, the youngsters did not bother to bunch closely behind their mothers. It is easy to say, watching this tableau, that gull and duck have reached some kind of peaceful accord with one another.

But then, a few hundred miles farther north of the eiders' nesting country, I have seen the eider ducklings being mercilessly harried by both herring gulls and blackbacks. I have watched attack after attack on the duckling strings, the tiny birds forced to bunch behind their mother so tightly that they looked like a single creature. I have seen herring gulls swoop down in one clean motion, seize a duckling that had strayed six inches from the maternal group and fly away, gulping as he went. I have seen duckling groups scattered hopelessly by gulls harassing them in their runs for the sea while the ducklings rammed themselves under stones, fell into rocky crevices, only to have the unlucky ones seized by gulls. Sometimes, only one duckling reaches the sea out of a family of ten.

Even more odd is the response of the female eider herself. Sometimes she fights for her ducklings, thrusting her body high up out of the water and lunging at overpassing gulls. Or she stands her ground on beach or gravel foreshore, quacking and leaping at the gulls. But other times, she just flies away and deserts her youngsters, and may not even be in sight as her family is decimated.

This is particularly noticeable along the northern shores of the Gulf of St. Lawrence where the eiders nest thickly in places and where there is heavy fishing boat traffic going to and from the shore. When the young ducklings are at sea there, their mothers are easily put to flight by passing boats, even though there is demonstrably no danger from them. Immediately, the blackbacks gather to harry the youngsters and it is one of the more pathetic sights of the shore to see the ducklings diving again and again until they are exhausted, half-drowned, and easy to kill.

So now, one is doubtful whether the eider duck is a fierce defender of her family or a cowardly deserter of her new brood. Then I get a final view of the eider duck that confuses me even further. A great black-backed gull makes an attack on an eider about to settle on her eggs which are placed in a fairly exposed position. The gull herself has her own nest not twenty feet away.

This time, the female eider defends her nest ferociously, charging forward, snapping her bill, and puffing out her feathers to make herself look twice as big as she really is. The gull is so nonplussed by such a savage response that she retreats momentarily. But then she reconsiders. It is, after all, only a duck that she is attacking. Yet the eider's defense prevails and the big gull is driven back.

Now comes the moment of real paradox. The gull walks (rather self-consciously, if I may humanize her for a moment) around the eider's nest to settle on her own eggs. The two incubating females sit within sight of each other. And I am left with the baffling question of when the eider can ever leave her nest if the gull is so determined destroy her eggs. If I wait long enough, I would almost certainly see the eiders hatch and go to sea safely, and the blackback, still feeding her nest-bound youngsters, paying no attention at all.

Perhaps the eider is just an odd character, unpredictable in her behavior. One last anecdote seems to confirm this. The eiders nest quite thickly in places among the great gull colony on Kent Island, and the ducks must walk considerable distances among gull nests to reach their own nests. It is a measure of their unpredictability, or confusion, or whatever, that they not infrequently lay some of their eggs in gull nests and that the gulls incubate them. I have never been around to see what happens when the eider hatches among gull chicks, but no better instance serves to illustrate the paradoxes and contradictions that abound for anyone watching the fascinating lives of the seabirds.

SEVEN: THE KILLING COUNTRY

I

The sea is brilliantly blue this day and the sky matches it. This is a moment that only the maritime region can produce in summer—bright sun, cool breeze, a brilliant clarity of air that reveals the sea horizon sharp as a knife edge. Where I am placed on the sea coast is not important, as long as seabirds are gathered somewhere nearby. It is their presence that transforms the collision of sea and land into sheer cosmos, birds above, sea beyond, land behind.

I use the word cosmos deliberately because this perfect day at this perfect place is in contrast to the chaos that once enveloped every place that seabirds gathered along every maritime shoreline. All the islands that I have mentioned were scenes of massacres scarcely believable to modern imaginations. But to contemplate them gives us one more insight into the survival of the seabird in America.

From almost the first day that the first white man set foot on these shores (whether he was an Irish monk or a Viking captain is scarcely important), the seabirds were hunted with a persistence and an efficiency which would long since have exterminated weaker creatures. These early hunters counted themselves lucky fellows to have their prey collected so conveniently in such great congregations; so easy to reach, so easy to kill, their bodies so easy to preserve. Besides, they provided such a bounty in eggs. It was a hunter's paradise. The birds, a repository of fresh meat, time and again saved starving fishermen and coastal folk from death.

To illuminate this age of killing, which began in earnest in the eighteenth century, reached a peak in the nineteenth, and gradually dies out in the twentieth, I would like to introduce Napoléon Comeau whom I have mentioned earlier. He was a nineteenth century French-Canadian who prowled the northern shores of the Gulf of St. Lawrence with a persistence and a genius bordering on the demonic. He killed for food as well as for sport, and his life exemplifies the ethic of an age we have outgrown, an age in which it was a wonder that any living thing survived.

Comeau's hunting life covered nearly half a century and there is no lifetime body count to measure his total kill. But he once shot one thousand murres in a day just for their feathers. He often boasted that he could bring down a dozen birds with one well-directed wing shot. One of his favorite hunting grounds was Perroquet Island, near the Straits of Belle Isle, the northern entrance to the gulf. From this island, he rarely returned with fewer than five hundred dead birds, usually eider ducks, murres, and puffins, and with a boatload of fresh eggs.

The aim of this kind of hunting was to kill, and kill, and keep on killing. During midsummer when scoters were molting along this shore and were made flightless, one of Comeau's tricks was to round up some friends in boats and go on a duck hunt. He and his friends banged tin cans, shouted and whistled, and rowed their boats around and around the helpless birds, forcing them to dive repeatedly. The panicked, exhausted birds eventually drowned by the hundreds.

It is easy for us, standing in the bright sunshine and watching the birds peacefully coming and going in their own cosmos, to imagine their place secure for the future. Less easy to imagine are the bloody summer slaughters at Funk Island where, since Viking times, men came to get their supplies of fresh meat for their great trans-Atlantic and Arctic journeys. This was the most punishing hunting of all, and it began with the most helpless seabird of all, the great auk. Funk Island was its headquarters for the western north Atlantic, and it is a tribute to the toughness of the great auk that it withstood such slaughter through the sixteenth, seventeenth, and eighteenth centuries. It kept returning to the island in its multiple thousands even while white and Indian hunters were camped there. Some of them penned the auks in rough stockades while they set up caldrons for rendering the fat birds down to their rich oil. The auks were so fat that their bodies could be used as fuel for the caldron fires. The great auks hung on as best they could in this climate of perpetual terror, but they were blotted out by the late eighteenth century on that island.

The disappearance of the great auks merely serves to dramatize the toughness and adaptability of auks generally, because after they had gone, the common murres persisted on the island, and their success on Funk paralleled the growth of the cod fishery off the coast of Labrador in the mid- to late nineteenth century.

On an earlier visit to the island, I had talked to old Newfoundland fishermen who could remember when Funk was surrounded by a score of schooners, a hundred men ashore slaughtering the birds for their summer meat. There was no compassion or sportsmanship in this hunt. The fishermen used short, flat paddles to smash down on the heads of the nesting murres. Like many of the auks, the murres stand fast at their nests to protect their eggs and nestlings when man approaches. Whether this is because they lack experience with landbound hunters or because it has proved to be the best survival device we cannot know. But for the paddle wielders, it was a kind of paradise since the birds nest densely together and a single paddle blow might kill half a dozen creatures. Funk Island, in those bloodthirsty years, yielded more than one hundred thousand birds annually until its population was brought down so low it was no longer worth a schooner's time to stop there.

Most of the auks are good to eat, and that was their misfortune. But the gannet, whose flesh is a little too strong and tough for the human palate, did not, for that reason, come through this era of unrestricted hunting in much better shape. Unfortunately, its flesh proved to be effective codfish bait. This fact alone brought the gannets of our maritime world to the point of extinction. By 1850, they were mostly gone. John James Audubon reached Bird Rock in the center of the Gulf of St. Lawrence in 1833, and counted about two hundred fifty thousand gannets still nesting there. His visit occurred just as the local fishermen were beginning to develop their great cod fishery in the surrounding Magdalen Shallows. The nearest available bait was gannet flesh.

This single rock island, which juts up starkly out of the sea in odd contrast to the mainly sandy Magdalen Islands nearby, provided about the same annual harvest of birds as Funk Island. The great American ornithologist, Arthur Cleveland Bent, once estimated that the rock colony kept about forty fishing vessels supplied with bait, which meant a kill of about one hundred thousand birds a year. The killings continued for twenty years and reduced the local population to one hundred fifty thousand birds. A lighthouse was built on the rock in 1887 by which time there were only about ten thousand birds left. By 1939, about one thousand regular breeders kept the summer colony just surviving.

The murres and the gannets were dying in their countless thousands, but one of the great delicacies of early men here was the kittiwake. If taken from the nest just before it is fledged, the nesting kittiwake makes one of the most delicious seabird dishes imaginable, as succulent and tender as squab with none of the strong, conventional fish flavor. The local people hunted them mercilessly, and no cliff was too steep for these rock-climbing hunters. Usually, they were able to skim almost every young bird from a cliff in one or two days' hunting because the kittiwake youngsters all come to maturity at roughly the same time.

The seabirds were easy to kill and died massively, but as their numbers diminished, the attention of the hunters turned gradually to the more difficult kills. These included the puffin, a bird which had wisely, if accidentally, made preparation for the arrival of the men by building deep burrows. It was possible for the hunters to dig out the puffins, but it was exhausting and not very profitable work.

Instead, they chose to imitate the puffin hunters of the Orkneys and the Faroes in northeastern Atlantic waters. There, the islanders had devised specialist techniques for killing their prey. One of the favorite was to cut a sapling up to fifteen feet long, then the hunter would lie on his back, the long stick gripped firmly in his hands and balanced between his legs. He looked back and up at the puffins whose habit it is to circle continually over any intruder to their domain. They fly so incautiously low that a skillful stick wielder can, with a powerful jerk of

(continued on page 177)

THE TERNERY

The Arctic tern is the world's greatest traveler, breeding far into the Arctic
and resting deep into the Antarctic. Its visit to North American shores is only
an ephemeral pause for a creature that may fly twenty-two thousand miles
every twelve months, that sees the Caribbean, the Azores, the Canaries, the
shores of Africa and South America, the desert islands, the Antarctic volcano
Erebus. But the Arctic tern carries the weight of its great travels lighly as
it touches the evening skies of northern shorelines with its singular grace.

The Arctic tern rides on wings designed by evolution, the master artist. Narrow and pointed for speed, they are supple-jointed for displaying to others of its kind and for diving abruptly into the sea when fishing, and they are perfectly proportioned for the human eye to marvel at as the tern passes overhead.

The nesting of the Arctic tern reflects the character of the bird itself—unpredictable and adaptable. In places where it nests close to the sea, as on Machias Seal Island in the Bay of Fundy, it may prefer bare rocks where its eggs, placed along the fault of a great block of stone, blend perfectly with granite and lichen. Or it may nest deep in the weeds and grass, dropping like a helicopter to the hidden hollow, since its legs are the shortest of all terns and are useful only for the most awkward hobbling on ground. And then, to surprise the watcher, the tern may gather nesting material and begin a new family on the bleached wreckage of an old dory. Or it may even decorate its nest on the beach with seaweed and the shells of clams and mussels.

At the beginning of the breeding season, the ternery moves from one uproar to another. A male will stake out a nesting site, fight off all comers, and this attracts a female who sees the place—not the male—as desirable. But to take occupation, she must submit to him, yield to his dominance, and this holds the two birds together. Male and female Arctic terns are indistinguishable to human eyes—and apparently to each other. One ornithologist has reported that they check each other's sex by pecking. If the pecked bird pecks back, it is a male. If it submits, it is a female. Thus the bond between the pair must be reinforced, and all during the courtship and nesting time the birds are constantly displaying, their emotions running to swift and unexpected peaks. One of the most common displays is courtship feeding. The male arrives at his territory with an offering of a fish, usually a small herring or a sand eel, rarely several fish at a time. . . .

He attempts to give the fish to the female who may ignore him and turn away while he bobs and bows and rearranges the offering. His embarrassment at being rejected is apparent to any nonscientific watcher, and it sometimes so overwhelms him that he drops the fish and flies off to get another. . . .

But if he is persistent, the female eventually recognizes the importance of his gift and she turns and takes it from him. With a supremely triumphant gesture, he raises his long and slender neck and the demonstration is complete. The entire ceremony may even occur in the air, the female flying ahead, her neck stretched forward, and the male following, holding the fish, his head dropped. Sometimes another bird will attempt to seize the fish and rapid chases follow. The significance of the fish gift is deep, if enduringly mysterious.

At Machias Seal Island, the young tern's chances of survival depend mostly on the weather. It has no land-bound enemies, except clumsy tourists, and few birds of prey visit the island. But rain, driving wind, and heavy seas with blowing spume decimate the chicks. After thirty days at the nest, they are able to fly and they form into juvenile flights that sweep back and forth across the ternery. Yet each youngster is able to find its way back to its individual territory.

[*Overleaf*]
With the breeding done, the chicks fledged, and the bond between the adult pairs weakening, the mood of the ternery changes. The courtships stop and the screeching fights end. The Arctic terns now face a long and leisurely migration to the southern hemisphere. Some may wander due east across the North Atlantic while others strike out down the center of the ocean. There is no hurry to reach their destination, which may be eleven thousand miles away.

his arms and shoulders, bring up the stick and break a puffin's wing as he passes. This method of hunting puffins, while seeming so arduous, was still popular in the 1960s. I once found more than a dozen of these sticks on one island where they were obviously still in annual use.

II

Frequently, man's depreciation of the seabird was involuntary. This was the age of the lighthouse, with its inevitable men and its almost always inevitable dogs. The lighthouse men were lonely and a dog provided the best company they could have. But a dog let loose in the middle of great nesting congregations of seabirds almost always goes berserk. He had never had such a fantastic opportunity for apparently endless killing, and there are many records of dogs becoming "psychotic" as a result of long sojourns on islands with seabird colonies.

The arrival of the white man in our maritime world brought disaster first to the most easily accessible seabirds. Wherever they bred close to shore, or on the shore itself, or gathered in great congregations before migration, breeding, or simply to guard their recently fledged youngsters, they were vulnerable. The gulls of the southern Bay of Fundy had an almost perfect arrangement with the pelagic and planktonic life of the great Passamaquoddy Bay system. The immense interchange of tidal waters there meant an almost constant upthrusting of planktonic life, along with millions of young herring hunting the plankton, and other larger fish hunting the herring in turn.

Once, I paused for an afternoon off the port of Campobello at the head of the Passamaquoddy system and watched one of these tidal overturns. The water was racing out of the bay, compressed between two islands, and its turbulence covered hundreds of acres. Stretched for almost as far as I could see on almost all sides were scores of thousands of gulls, screaming and squabbling over the incredibly rich hunting being proffered them. Breaking the water all around me were other hunters I could not identify, and in the distance I saw the clean sleek black backs of a trio of whales breaking the surface.

This area was always a paradise for gull hunting besides being headquarters for their breeding. Traditionally, gulls once nested on the steep cliffs of Grand Manan Island as well as on Kent Island, a few miles off Grand Manan's shores. There, they gathered in what was perhaps the greatest single herring gull colony in the world. There, they tolerated the summer visits of scores of Indians who preyed on them for their eggs and feathers. In this environment, they maintained some kind of equilibrium with their hunters.

What they could not stand was the growing numbers of white men settling Grand Manan. They could not stand the import of raccoons and other egg-loving animals to the island by man. They could not stand the growth in popularity of gull feathers in the millinery trade.

Gradually, during the nineteenth century, their great uproarious breeding colonies along the cliffs of Grand Manan were silenced, one by one. Gradually, on Kent Island—a better sanctuary because no mammal ever reached it—they resorted to the strange trick of nesting and roosting in trees in an effort to escape the egg and feather hunters. There, incredibly, they did hang on all during the heaviest hunting. There, they were finally rescued when the island was bought by a Rockefeller and presented to Bowdoin College as a permanent sanctuary and scientific research station.

I am concerned with seabirds but watching them in their many fascinating habitats, I am constantly reminded how closely their lives sometimes intermingle with other birds of the shore and of the land. It was not just seabirds who suffered during the period of the great hunt. Napoléon Comeau estimated that in 1885, a total of sixty thousand willow ptarmigans were shot along 175 miles of Quebec shoreline.

The ptarmigan is a fecund bird, unlike the relatively slow-breeding seabirds, so this figure is perhaps not as startling as the fifty thousand to seventy thousand eider ducks that were killed each year along the coasts of Newfoundland. They were shot with an astonishing variety of weapons, including blunderbusses, American Civil War muskets, lethally designed guns called Long Toms, and even cannons on occasion. There were many records of three hundred to four hundred birds being killed in a single shot of a large-bore weapon. It is, perhaps, only partially consoling to reflect that the mortality of the hunters was high too because their hunting equipment was notoriously unreliable and dangerous.

Seabird and landbird thus merged into the hunt and became part of the common history of which we witnessed the tail end. The Quebec shore hunters regularly set traps on the tops of poles. One of Comeau's friends regularly set five traps for this winter hunting and he customarily caught one hundred or more snowy owls, dozens of gray and long-eared owls, and uncountable gyrfalcons, peregrine falcons, and jays. He never harvested less than one thousand pounds of bird flesh a year. But this was just one hunter. Hundreds of pole traps waited for the winter birds of that nineteenth-century shore.

III

As I move from colony to colony, I cannot help noticing the almost total absence of any normal predators of these bird bazaars. I note that their behavior *suggests* the possible arrival of a peregrine falcon, eagle, skua, or jaeger. But none of these predators, except one tantalizing glimpse of a fast-flying hawk in the trough of a wave, is given to me.

It takes real imagination, therefore, to see this entire seabird world at the mercy of countless winged hunters. Previously, I had seen gyrfalcons operating in the far north on a murre colony and had been dazzled by their boisterous, exuberant daily attacks into great curtains of moaning murres. They cut down one or two birds every day, frequently killing just for the fun of it.

This must have been the situation on these islands. But the hawks and eagles are long gone. The fate of the birds of prey can be found, once again, in the histories. The nineteenth century saw hawks and eagles as fair game for everybody. One of Napoléon Comeau's favorite tricks was to kill bald eagles with a stick when they became so gorged on salmon flesh that they could not fly. He lived in a time when the golden eagle was common, so numerous along this shore that he once boasted of shooting three of them in a morning.

Now, with their natural predators almost gone—the eagles and falcons and other birds of prey have been almost obliterated by the greatest predator of all, man himself—the destruction of the seabirds is more or less over. Their numbers are stabilized, or are increasing, their futures seem certain, unless some new ecological disaster, hitherto unpredicted, visits their world. Thousands of eiders and murres may still fall to hunters' guns, illegal hunting this, but their numbers are now so great, the protection of their sanctuaries so complete, that the survival of their populations is no longer an issue. If there is regret here, it is that the peregrine falcons, the eagles, and the gyrfalcons have probably gone forever. Man has been able to accept the seabird, but he is still uncertain about creatures that kill his chickens and silence his songbirds.

EIGHT: FINALE

I

The year of the seabird ends, at least for the land-bound watcher. The signs of this are all around me, long before the first mists and gales of fall begin. The mood of the shore has become somber, foreboding, and evocative of revolutionary changes to come. I have stood on the tidal flatlands of sand in the Bay of Fundy, in the late summer, and watched several thousand sandpipers sweeping in a dark hissing clot along the edge of the water. They were then moving gradually south, having seized that brief moment when the Arctic permitted them a place in its six weeks of thaw and bloom. They passed me then among birds of both land and sea who were still breeding. Now, with the fall at hand, I can watch these tiny migrants again, a thousand miles or more down the coast, still beach-hopping toward the south.

The sandpipers are a small triumph of survival because, in past centuries, they were not only esteemed for the cooking pot but were also extraordinarily easy to exterminate. Shooting blinds were common all along the Fundy shore, a favorite migration feeding ground for these little shorebirds. If a gunner could bring down one bird, the entire flock would turn back to flutter over the victim and the gunner merely had to keep firing until he had killed the last bird.

The extermination of shorebirds is a melancholy fact since so many of them have failed to return to their ancient numbers and one, at least, the Eskimo curlew, is nearly extinct. But I like to watch the sandpipers today because they speak of their triumph over man and a changing world as they provide a curtain-raising spectacle for the fall migration of seabirds back into the vastness of their winter ranges.

As the murres begin forming up into migration armies to plunge into the sea from Funk Island, and so float south in the grip of the Labrador current, they provide another spectacle of recovery—the most dramatic among all the seabirds in this region. At the turn of the century, there were close to zero populations throughout our maritime world. But once their recovery began, it was irresistible. By 1934, there were twenty thousand murres on Funk Island, and thirty thousand by 1945. All during this period they remained a prime resource for fishermen who salted their flesh and preserved their eggs. But there were fewer fishermen now, and the whalermen who had once gone to the Arctic in their thousands had disappeared completely.

With the end of World War II, the recovery of the murres became an avalanche, spurred by the fact that human conditions were changing sharply and prosperity was coming to people who had been destitute. New bait, new foods, new needs were spreading through the societies of the shore. There were one hundred thousand murres on the island by 1952; three hundred thousand by 1956. The recovery turned into a geometric miracle with an estimated one million birds packing the island by 1959. When I last visited Funk in the sixties, there could have been as many as one and a half million murres there, a dense, stinking, roaring mass of birds, howling their defiance at two centuries of persecution.

With the summer coming to an end, the murres form up in their armies and start moving out to sea. Simultaneously, the adults are molting completely, seizing this one brief opportunity between the end of their parental responsibilities and the beginning of their winter hunting.

II

The recovery of the gannets is scarcely less spectacular. After being driven to the brink of extinction throughout the maritime region, they repopulated Funk Island after an absence of more than one hundred years and made it their northernmost colony in North America. Eventually, they even displaced the murres from the best breeding "heights," a low hummock of rock on the island. The rebuilding of their colonies at Baccalieu and Bird Rock are even more dramatic, their numbers rising from scant hundreds to the scores of thousands. When I pass up through the cool woodlands leading to the colony at Bonaventure Island in late summer, I always do so with anticipation. This is one of the fastest-increasing colonies. The birds are repopulating so rapidly they are pushing their nesting area back beyond the cliff tops, cutting into forest territory, and killing the trees by the density of their occupation.

There, looking down across the magnificent broad sweep of the open Atlantic from the heights of the island, I see an open, fieldlike area of grass where once the gannets had so thickly occupied the slopes that they permanently displaced the forest. If their present rate of increase continues, they will probably repopulate all this grassland.

Now, in this terminal moment of the year, the nestling gannets are lined up awaiting their departure. Like so many of the other young seabirds who must make a massive adjustment to a new way of life without much, or any, assistance from their parents, the young gannets are about as fat as they can be. They are uniformly dressed in mottled white on dark gray—pepper-and-salt plumaging it has been called—and the family bonds either have been broken down or are attenuated. The adult gannets return regularly to the tops of the cliffs and some of them still bring food to nestlings. But now, the nestlings are almost as big as the adults, and their violent stabbing motions with their sharp beaks down the throats of their parents look positively dangerous for the older birds.

Their fatness evokes other ages when this was time for the mass slaughter of the young birds on both sides of the Atlantic, the plump youngsters providing excellent winter food for the men on the islands. But already the fat is being consumed, and the thousands of youngsters will lose tons of flesh over these days in August, about one pound for every bird, bringing each down to an average weight of seven pounds.

By the time the youngsters have begun leaping off the cliffs for their first clumsy flights down to the sea, the adults are already well spread, some of them hundreds of miles to the south on their way to the shores of Virginia, the Carolinas, Florida, and the Gulf of Mexico. Quite suddenly one day, the cliffs are empty except for half a dozen herring gulls dozing among the whitened remains of the gannetry. Mist rises from the blue sea; a quick gale hisses into the spruces behind. The gannets' year is done.

III

The herring gulls have had rather more mixed success in recovering from ancient massacres. They have never earned the respect of man. While they have been helped by the increase in fish processing plants and small, motor-powered boats, finding suitable nesting areas has remained their prime problem. They were never able to make much of a comeback on Grand Manan Island itself since it has become so well populated by egg-loving raccoons. Kent Island is their great off-shore landing ground, and once the hunting stopped there, they could come down from the trees and begin nesting on the ground. They do so now in the scores of thousands. I have always fancied there is special justice in the presence of Kent Island. Without it, the herring gulls of the Passamaquoddy would have had trouble surviving at all. Their persecution is not ended; they need this sanctuary. Several efforts have been made along the mainland to bring their numbers down to "manageable levels." They are accused, with truth, of being eider duck killers. They frequently catch other young seabirds. They harass petrels returning to their islands at night. And as a final outrage to man, they are inveterate harvesters of blueberries just a few days before man himself considers them fit to eat. Kent Island, under the protection of the conservationists, has a population of upward of sixty thousand birds. They may no longer nest in trees there but they have not lost their liking for roosting in trees. One of the more pleasant sights of the island is to stand on its eastern shores, looking into the eye of the setting red sun, and watch dozens of herring gulls standing like statues in the spruces. The trees are long since dead, killed by the sheer density of gull occupation, and the gulls stand in them in silhouette like strange, tapered fruit.

Their departure, in the fall of the year, is not quite like that of any of the other seabirds. First, not being true seabirds, they have none of the drive to get free of the land. They are half of the shore, half of the sea, and they reflect this in their abandonment of their breeding places. Nobody knows how their territorial arrangements are worked out, but it is a strict arrangement. Some gulls, particularly the older ones, migrate hardly at all. Their total winter movement may be a short flight from Kent Island to the wharves and fish plants of Grand Manan. It may be no flight at all, but a constant winter prowling of the great Passamaquoddy Bay area. It may be moving a score of miles from a breeding place on a Newfoundland cliff to fishing grounds along a suitable shoreline.

These are the lucky ones, or perhaps just the old ones. The territory of the gullery cannot take thousands of new lives added so suddenly to a changing season. The bulk of the younger birds must migrate. It is a migration with a special stamp on it. Herring gulls drift inland to the Great Lakes, or they wander along the shores of the St. Lawrence River. They drift down the Atlantic shore and end up on city dumps anywhere they can find enough food. Some go clear down to the Gulf of Mexico and join frigate birds and boobies, pelicans and ibis, in totally alien hunting grounds. They do not migrate so much as they explode into a great dispersion which spreads them as widely as possible from the place of their birth.

IV

The recovery of the herring gull is contentious for some bird lovers. But the triumph of the puffin provokes no arguments. He is, you might say, the universally admired seabird. I am not one of his special fans, except to be an admirer of those extraordinary beak decorations. He is, as I have said, rather a humorless fellow, but the bird has an hypnotic hold over the imaginations of seabird lovers. Special expeditions are organized to see nothing but puffins. They respond, as best they can, I suppose, by parading on the rocks around the blinds. They put on small comic shows of landing and taking off for the assembled photographers.

The puffin never suffered as badly as the murres from the exploitation of man. Because he was always able to dig deep burrows and because he is generally a more wary bird, he was never brought down as low during the time of the great hunters. From his position of relative strength, he has made new colonizing ventures. When two American ornithologists, Harold S. Peters and Thomas D. Burleigh of the U.S. Fish and Wildlife Service, examined the birds of Newfoundland in the 1940s, they recorded no puffins from Great Island on the east coast. Today, scores of thousands of puffins smother the island from end to end, and have so well riddled it with burrows that it takes considerable physique to walk from one end of the island to the other. The puffin occupation is so complete that the island is studded with abandoned "cities," where the digging has caused the soil to collapse, as if it had covered an overzealously dug coal mine. Then the puffins desert the area and move on to new places, perhaps even more ancient cities where collapse has occurred, the burrows filled in with eroded soil and mud, the grass grown thickly over them, and the site ready to be dug all over again.

Now, in August or September, it is possible to visit many of the puffinries and find them apparently deserted. The adults have gone to sea and are dispersing. They, like the murres, are molting. They will soon drop the great ornamentations from their beaks. Behind them they have left their scores of thousands of youngsters alone in their burrows. The young puffins, meantime, are losing the last of their nestling down. The first feathers of their juvenile plumage, all the wing and tail feathers, are growing rapidly despite the fact that the callow birds have been deserted and are not feeding. Like the gannets, they have been fattened and can fast for a week or ten days. Some of them appear warily at the entrances of their burrows. But they are scared of gulls and other enemies, and it is only on islands like Machias Seal, where the gulls have been kept off, that they venture out into the sun and wander around the rocks.

On the more northern islands, their departure is unseen. They leave the burrows at night, tumble over rocks, or down cliff faces into the

water, and so are free to begin their new lives in the plastic world of
the sea. That sea, however, may be becoming less hospitable to puffins and their kind. There are disturbing reports from the North Atlantic of recent and catastrophic population crashes, particularly on
the Scottish island of St. Kilda, where puffin numbers have plunged
from three million to 250,000. On this side of the ocean, puffin colonies on the north shore of the Gulf of St. Lawrence have declined 35
percent since 1965. Razorbills likewise seem to be in trouble. The
cause of all this is a mystery to scientists, but they harbor dark sus-
picions that pollution of the sea with toxic chemicals, and perhaps
intensive commercial fishing pressure, are somehow to blame.

V

The Leach's petrels resemble the puffin in that they never suffered
grievously during man's occupation of this maritime region. They began as birds of mystery, and they remain mysterious. There are no
comprehensive or accurate stories of their early numbers. Being nocturnal visitors, they aroused no special interest or attention among the
early settlers. But they do appear to be increasing in some areas today,
and decreasing in others. The Peters and Burleigh survey recorded five
hundred pairs of them on Gull Island in the 1940s. But today, this
island hosts perhaps as many as a million of them, certainly forming
the largest Leach's petrel colony anywhere in the world. They can
also be found on the cliffs at Bonaventure where they seem to be
increasing. They have been forced as far north as Funk Island which
may be new breeding territory for them. They are declining on Kent
Island. They occur on various small islands along the Nova Scotian
coast, and Machias Seal Island, with its lighthouse, provides one of the
only places where they are visible in their nightly visits. But the fate of
the species, its life history details, remains difficult to pin down. The
young petrels, we know, are abandoned in their burrows. Old timers
swore that the young petrel spent the whole winter in the burrow.
They are, indeed, reluctant to leave the burrows and have been found
in them as late as October. By that time, their parents must be thousands of miles away, perhaps even off the coast of Africa itself.

That other great wanderer, the kittiwake, is less mysterious and more successful. Certainly one of the most heavily hunted of all the seabirds, it had been brought down to as few as five thousand on Newfoundland's Green Island by the 1940s. But today, there are fifty thousand or sixty thousand of them on the steep cliffs there. No egg or nestling hunters have either the desire or nerve to tackle such dangerous hunting when TV dinners are available. These gregarious little gulls disappear from their breeding cliffs suddenly and disperse. They are true seabirds and while some hunt the shores of Greenland, others will wander as far east as Russia and winter at the edge of the advancing ice.

The ducks appear to be coming back everywhere, despite the systematic shooting of them along the eastern coast of Newfoundland. This is an illegal hunt that the wildlife authorities do not interfere with since the ducks are able to accept the annual sixty thousand bird casualty rate without losing numbers. The Newfoundlanders are still not rich people. It is argued that a duck in every pot is as good a way of satisfying the primal urge to hunt as anything else.

With Napoléon Comeau and his friends now well gone, the scoters are free to gorge on the herring spawn in growing flocks along the shores of the northern Gulf. The eiders, which had been kept relatively far north by the heavy hunting in the southern maritime region, have gradually moved south, extending their range closer to human contact. They have taken over Hay Island, in the southern Bay of Fundy, and are appearing in increasing numbers on islands down into the Gulf of Maine.

The year is at its end and the seabirds have gone. The year is over for me too, because I do not have the stamina to remain at their bleak and empty breeding places waiting for their return seven or eight months hence. I don't know much more about them than when I started. The measurement of the experience remains an emotional one, and therefore, immeasurable.

Once, after writing about gannets, I mentioned that I could not recall ever having read a lyrical line about the bird, and conjectured that this was because all the best poets, like Shakespeare, lived inland or in countries where gannets were never seen. I was politely rebuked by a learned Michigan man who noted that an elegiac poem, "Seafarer," an early English effort written about eleven hundred years ago, was very specific in its attempt to convey a lyric line about the gannet and other seabirds.

> *There I heard naught save the harsh sea*
> *And ice-cold wave, at whiles the swan cries,*
> *Did for my games the gannet's clamor,*
> *Sea-fowls' loudness was for me laughter,*
> *The mews' singing all my mead-drink.*

The strangeness of their world, the clamor of their voices, the overpowering presence of them in their colonies, all combine to permanently score the memories of men. The seabird remains to the end, out of reach, mysterious, unfathomable, as he heads south and east, away from the land and into the deep ocean. As he disappears, he deserves a toast to his safe return to land the following spring, and his survival on earth forever.